Growth Marketing: Strategy & Execution Bootcamp For Startups

Gaurav Sanjiv Kalangan

Published by Gaurav Sanjiv Kalangan, 2024.

Also by Gaurav Sanjiv Kalangan

Learn Options Strategies Options Basics & Greeks For Stock Trading By Technical Analysis
Bitcoin, Altcoins & ICOs Learn the Basics of Digital Coins from Zero
Time Management This Is How I Work 300 Percent Faster
How To Build And Implement A Winning Pricing Strategy
Networking For Introverts: Gracefully Exiting A Conversation
Accounting 101: Learn Cost Accounting From A To Z
Growth Marketing: Strategy & Execution Bootcamp For Startups

Table of Contents

Copyright

Published by Gaurav Sanjiv Kalangan

Copyright © 2024 Gaurav Sanjiv Kalangan

All rights reserved.

Distributed by Gaurav Sanjiv Kalangan

Growth Marketing: Strategy & Execution Bootcamp For Startups

Design and composition by Gaurav Sanjiv Kalangan Cover design by Gaurav Sanjiv Kalangan For permission credits.

To offset the number of trees consumed in the printing of our books, Gaurav Sanjiv Kalangan donates a portion of the proceeds from each printing to the Arbor Day Foundation. Gaurav Sanjiv Kalangan has replaced over 50 trees since 2022.

First Edition

I dedicate this to the dreamers, healers, and givers who deliver value through art and invention, expression, and creation. With all my love.

About

"I know what my startup's goals are but I have no idea how to get there"

In the field, the truth is most startups die from being unable to materialize their goals into actual results. Too much strategy and too little action. The fact is that goal seeking is an applied skill; it takes time, practice and mistakes to get really good at it and its nuances:

1. Whether a product already exists or not, how do you determine the path to reaching your goals?
2. How do you set goals?
3. What is the simplest way to gain a heuristic understanding of every moving piece contributing to your desired bottom line?

After helping dozens of companies systemize their approach to growth through advisory engagements, accelerator mentorship and hands-on workshops, the Growth Models & Goalkeeping masterclass was created to help transfer those skills on-demand.

The goal of this masterclass is to share my emotional, psychological and logical approach to designing growth systems with you so you can apply that approach to your use case.

Avoid Big Capital Expenditures 1

As a startup, you need to avoid big capital expenditures, big investments that take a lot of cash because you don't have a lot of cash in the beginning and you need to be more agile with the things that you invest in. So let's walk through a few examples of what those big capital expenditures might be. One example is a website. When people set up a startup, they think, well, I definitely need a website. I need to get some sort of credibility out there on the Internet. I need to get some branding and put something up on a website. But let me tell you, as somebody who used to make a lot of money selling websites and selling them for 10, 20 thousand dollars, something I've learned along the way is that it isn't necessary.

You can build an entire marketing system that gets results, gets sales, gets leads for you without needing to take that five thousand dollars, ten dollars, ten thousand dollars, whatever, and sink it into a sunk investment. That is a website because a website is an investment that pays dividends. In the long run, it's not going to pay for itself immediately. There are ways to get results quickly and more effectively than a website. And I'm going to show you what those are. So, for example, one thing that I typically recommend for startups is that they start with LinkedIn ads. Now, when you run LinkedIn ads, you don't need a website. You don't even need a landing page. You just go straight to advertising.

You take that money that you would have put towards your website, your logo, your copywriting, etc. You put it directly into the market with ads and that's going to lead directly to customer acquisition. Now, let me just walk you through a few examples of results I've got. So I was able to get views for three sets. That's actually the minimum that you can pay on LinkedIn to have potential customers. read your chapter. And I was able to do that. I'm able to get hundreds of people, potential buyers reading my chapter, three cents each. There's no website. There's no fixed investment at all. I just go straight to advertising. Other examples. I'm able to get free trial sign ups.

Twenty three dollars. You can get, quote, requests for like forty fifty dollars. And that's immediately going to your sales pipeline. It's not. Require that you sink a lot of money into some big expensive retainer or website or anything, you just go straight to the advertising. I'm able to hit target customers' inboxes with messages for 17 cents each. You realize how ridiculously cheap that is. I mean, if you want to send direct mail or something that's going to cost, the printing alone will probably be more than 17 cents to get those postcards, those mailboxes out there. And often the way that I make this effective is I capture the leads. I capture the interest in LinkedIn itself using their native form.

I don't need to pay a web developer to build a form on a website or a landing page, optimize it, test it. LinkedIn has already done that. They've already figured it out. They've already automated. They have already given you the capability to do all of this without any programming skill, without any design skill and being able to target specifically your target audience and get results this effectively. So let me ask you, if you have five thousand dollars in your bank account, would you rather a five thousand dollar website where you have to continuously add content yourself through the blog? You need to continuously update it. You need to continue to maintain it.

You need to pay for hosting. You need to pay for domain registration. OK, so don't get me wrong, a website is a good investment in the long run. OK, but if you're strapped for cash and I don't know what stage your startup is at, if you're if you're doing OK and you're a bit established, maybe have a few dozen customers.

OK, great. Invest in your website. But when you're first starting out and when you're thinking about where most of your money should be invested, you need to think in terms of marketing systems. Not nice to have items like a website. OK, so scenario one is you get this website and you've got to keep feeding it. You have all these maintenance costs or scenarios where you get 50 people requesting calls with your sales team.

OK, so I'm assuming there it's going to cost about 50 dollars to get somebody to request a, quote, consultation, request a demo, maybe sign up for free trial, which would you rather would you rather a pipeline of customers, potential customers that are actively in conversations about buying your product or five thousand dollars website that could potentially lead to people finding you on the website through the Internet, which they probably won't because you're going to need to continuously pay for search engine optimization other in terms of money or time. So I just think the best approach when you're a startup is to take the most direct route to getting customers rather than getting distracted by things like a big fancy website.

OK, I'm going to walk you through another example of what I'm talking about. So I was doing research in one of my jobs, looking at data for thousands of e-commerce sellers. And what I wanted to figure out was. Who's actually making serious money, who's making the millions and is really establishing a solid business that they can invest in. And one of the trends I noticed was that a lot of these really successful e-commerce sellers were on Amazon. That's where the bulk of their sales were coming from. It was not their own website. It was in a marketplace. So Amazon builds the website. They build the template for what your sales page looks like.

They control what the font is. You don't have to pay for hosting. It's all there for you. Those are the people that were making the millions, the tens of millions now. Shopify, you have to build your own website, you have to build your own brand, you have to send people to your website, you have to generate your traffic. Now, listen, I'm not saying shop. Shopify is really successful. Shopify sellers are really successful. But as a startup, it's just much, much easier if you focus less on building websites and more on actually generating sales. And I think one of the reasons in the kind of small mid stages why Amazon sellers tend to be so successful is because it's focused on selling.

When you have a marketplace and you put your listing up there with your products, the focus becomes less about how do I do these things that are fun? How do I come up with a cool name, a cool brand, a cool mailing list, all this kind of fun Brandee stuff? Instead, it focuses you on selling because a lot of that stuff when you're building a website are distractions there things that could potentially pay off in the long run. But in the beginning, you need to be proving that you can generate sales. And by having an Amazon listing instead of a website, you're focusing on what actually generates results.

Avoid Big Capital Expenditures 2

Some other examples of big capital expenditures to avoid, particularly in the early stages, would be something like paying a PR agency a retainer of five thousand dollars per month. Don't get me wrong, I think PR is a great way to generate awareness very quickly. Maybe you get a big funding round and you really want to get attention from potential partners and customers. But when you're in startup mode, five thousand dollars a month is a lot of money. I mean, that's a full time employee that you could have constantly doing stuff for you eight hours a day. So sinking five thousand dollars into a retainer may potentially lead to future customers down the road. Probably not the most direct way to get customers now.

So other examples that I consider sunk capital expenditures and, you know, there may be exceptions to this, but in general, one of the most common mistakes I see is just way too much focus on what I would call inbound content marketing or kind of the idea that your startup needs to be a journalistic entity, your startup know, unless you're in the publicity industry or you're in the business of creating a magazine, chances are your company is not going to be as effective at generating content as people that are actually doing that as their job. So, for example, if you're selling software, you're not in the business of creating newspaper articles. If you're selling widgets on Amazon, that's not your game.

You're not you're not a fashion magazine. So let's avoid some of the inbound content marketing stuff because it's too indirect, takes too much time. It's a great investment if you want to dabble in it and build something. But when I'm in startup mode, I'm interested in getting money, I'm interested in getting customers, and I'm interested in getting them this month or next month, this quarter, not one year down the road, because we're in survival mode, we're in pivot mode. Let's get results. Let's see what doesn't get results so we can pivot quickly. Can't do that when you're investing too much time in building a content generating machine.

So, for example, common advice out there. Write lots of blog articles. That takes a lot of time. And if it doesn't take a lot of time it is going to take a lot of money. So, for example, let's say you pay a writer five hundred dollars to do a blog post that may generate search results. Well, you can probably not get much results with a single blog article, but I can guarantee you, if you think five hundred dollars in the LinkedIn ads, in the Google ads, in Facebook ads and do it correctly, you're going to get a result. OK, maybe in the beginning you won't be profitable because you targeted the wrong people or you bid too high, but.

You're going to get results with a blog, it's hit or miss, you don't know that that blog is even going to break, even in terms of the amount of time, the amount of money you invested in other examples, podcasts, people say to start a podcast. Yeah, that's great. If you're in it for the long haul, you're planning to be around for five years. You know what your focus is? Build a podcast, build a following. But I can tell you from the get go, that is not going to get you results. Now, I'm going to talk about some strategies later that can get results, which is borrowing credibility from people that have already done these things like blogs and podcasts.

But from the beginning, unless that's your business, your core businesses, I'm going to run a podcast. I'm going to run a YouTube channel. Don't do it. At least not in the beginning. OK, YouTube channels. Another example. Yes, you can make money from YouTube channels. Yes, you can build your brand on YouTube. Yes, it's going to help your credibility and it's going to lubricate the sales process because people are already familiar with you. But that is a big investment that takes a lot of time to build that followership. That should not be your game plan as a startup. There are easier, cheaper, faster ways to acquire customers.

And inbound content in general is a machine that takes a lot of momentum to get going. OK, it is. It's a snowball. It's not going to get you results tomorrow. So let me ask you, which would you rather have a cold email that generates a meeting with a 30 million dollar C suite team immediately? Or. A one year commitment to generate blog content that may be ROIC positive in the second year of investment. I think it's pretty simple, right? When you're in startup mode, you would much rather have a sales call than an investment that can theoretically pay off if you keep investing in it. If you keep doubling down on this first example to call the email to get a 30 million dollars Sweetin, I did this and I'm going to show you exactly how that was done.

And I just want you to think about how ridiculously cheap it is, OK? I pay fifty dollars a month for this old email tool. I bought a list, an email list that cost, I think maybe two hundred two hundred fifty dollars and then I just ran it automatically. I don't I don't need to pay an SDR. I don't need to pay for ongoing ads. I don't need to invest in five hundred dollars or spend three hours writing some long blog content. I just ran the cold email. Exactly the people that I want to buy my product and you can do it even cheaper than that. OK, I bought a list. You can make your own list. You could just go grab a list from an association website of the people that you want buying your product and run the cold email campaign.

It's cheap and it's effective and it leads immediately to sales like inbound content marketing where it's just indirect, and takes a lot of time. You're going to get a lot of people that are not qualified to use your product here with an email. You can target exactly who you think will buy the product. OK, so here's what my Dema looks like, it was all automated, I'm able to send this to thousands of people, send it to a couple hundred today. And it just had a subject line, ideas and feedback for and then after the form was the company name. And I said hi. And then I'd put in my first name as a variable in this email tool called Unless I'm reaching out because I thought you might want some free advice.

And then I established the credibility of myself as an individual, as a consultant, and then bam, I got a message from the CEO, this 30 million dollar business say, yeah, I want to hear what you have to say. I want to have a meeting. The rest of the C suite. We get in on the meeting there. That's a sales call. That's how you generate sales and it's all done automatically. This tool is called Timeless. I'm not an affiliate or anything, use whatever email tool you want. Mail shake, step one, simple, simple email. That's just the first name as the ideas and feedback for the company name. And then I put their first name in the greeting here and then I send it to email. Five days later, it's all fully automated.

I just uploaded a whole list there. Now, you know, you're going to have some challenges if you're in business to consumer marketing. Don't worry, there's other ways you can do it when you're doing consumer emails, you can do message ads that are paid for. You can get into people's inboxes either way. I don't I'm not telling you to do anything malicious here. And I just want you to think about this for a second. I don't need a designer. I don't need a developer. I don't need to hire a copywriter. I just sent a short email. It's got my photo. You don't even need your photo. And all I'm doing is getting people to respond to say, yes, I'm interested.

That's how you generate sales quickly. OK, another thing, companies will want to invest in office space a lot of the time this is because they're small. They want to be perceived as more credible. Don't do it. Why, if you see that money into an office now, OK, maybe it's necessary, maybe there are nuances here where people need to walk in your office depending on what kind of startup you are. But if you're a consultant, if you're an e-commerce business, if you're pretty much anything, nobody cares about your fancy office space. It's just going to be a waste of money. Let's focus on generating and generating revenue and less on big capital expenditures like this.

All right, another thing that I see is startups that become obsessed with automation and scalability. Before they've even proven that there's a proof of concept there, that they know that this can actually generate sales. So automation is great and a lot of people, even one person businesses, generate a million dollars because they invest in automation. The problem I see is they'll invest tons of money into some automation software because they're talked into it, because a lot of the people that control the share voice in the Internet are software companies. And I'm from and don't get me wrong, I'm not biased against software. But you don't need to spend thousands of dollars on some sort of automation software. You can hire people.

You can pay somebody five dollars an hour, ten dollars an hour, whatever, you can get them locally, you can get them on five or you can get them up to work and find them on Craigslist. I had tons of people in the Philippines working for me happily in the Philippines because I found them on Craigslist. They needed money. I needed workers, bing, bam, boom. That was easy now when I worked, or when I lived in Norway. Excuse me. What I noticed was that a lot of things were automated. You go to return your bottles for recycling. There's an automation machine. A lot of the change that's produced when you buy something was automated. And this was this way years ago, something like ten years ago before this became mainstream.

And the reason is because the labor costs are really high in Norway. Ridiculously high, super expensive to hire people, so that's why they invested in these automation tools. But today we're working in a global market. You can hire employees anywhere and you don't have to hire them in places where labor is super expensive. So why not just get somebody to do the job instead of getting a machine to do the job? Because automation machinery is more ROIC positive. The bigger you get, the more you've scale. But in the beginning, it is more versatile, more agile to just get somebody to do the job because there's going to be a lot of tweaking. It's going to be a lot of changes. There's going to be a lot of variability in what you're doing in the beginning, probably more custom tailored orders to customers in the beginning.

Later, once you've scaled up, then start thinking about automation because the benefits accrue more strongly when you have a large user base, a large customer base. So generally, what I'm saying here at a high level is that when you're a startup, you need to focus on the state income statement, let's maximize sales, maximize revenue, minimize expenses, especially non operational expenses. Big investments are often a very bad idea. When you're a large company or mid-sized company, things start to change. You're less interested in revenue, more interested in assets that are going to produce revenue efficiently in the long run. So there's a twist that happens as you grow where you need to shift your mindset from sales to assets. And I'm just going to show you a few examples of what these look like, so.

In the beginning as a startup and these are general rules, OK, there's going to be exceptions. I know people reading this, you're probably going to start resisting some of the things I'm saying, largely because there's a lot of propaganda out there that just wants you to spend money and time on things you don't need to. But if we take a look here, what are the things that generate sales, outbound demand generation? If you're in business, the business and consumer marketing, its outbound performance, marketing, things like Leegin Forms. We have them on Facebook, we have them on LinkedIn. You can do very, very targeted ads on Twitter. You can do it on Quora.

These types of things are going to get you results now rather than tomorrow. Paper click advertising. Very good at hitting people that are actively looking for a solution. They're in that buying mindset. It's going to generate sales quickly. The other thing that you can do, and I'm going to go into more detail on this later, is instead of building your own brand, you borrow other people's brands, you borrow their credibility, latch yourself onto them, associate with them, participate in their content to give you more credibility and get you more visibility. Cold email, extremely cheap, extremely efficient, extremely automated in a cheap way that doesn't require big investment and get sales immediately.

Now, then there's a big shift that happens when you're out of startup mode and rather large company. What matters now is less about sales. It's more about asset management. You've built up a brand, you've built up credibility, built up a customer list. Let's manage those assets. Let's manage those channels. So now it's more about your branding. It's more about brand management. It's more about owned channels. It's about your website. It's about your podcast. It's about your big event that you've built up for your company. It's about awareness campaigns for branding on a wide scale. It's about entertainment. It's about being top of mind when the need arises.

That's not important. When you're a startup, you're not trying to hit people who may have a need in the future. You're going to be trying to hit people that have a need now. And if they don't, you can stimulate them so that they will respond. Now, different when you're a big company, you're thinking of longer time horizons, bigger scale, you're thinking inbound content machinery, and you're focusing a lot on research rather than just agile experimentation. So there's a big shift that happens. Don't get confused. Don't confuse what works for large companies with what's going to work for you now as a startup.

Borrow Credibility, Don't Build It

One of the most important things you need to do as a startup is borrow credibility. Don't try to build it. Yes, in the long run, you're going to build a brand, you're going to build credibility, but in the beginning, why bother? There are already people, there are already brands, there are already organizations that have credibility, that have influence, that have giant mailing lists, that have followers that trust them. Why start from Ground Zero when you can piggyback off of the credibility that's already out there? I think this is some of the poorest advice that I hear out there is you need to build a brand. You need to build a mailing list. You don't need to do that stuff, OK? It takes decades in a lot of cases to build a brand. OK, you don't even know if your business is going to survive the next year.

Let's forget about what's going to happen 15 years down the road. Yeah, OK. When you're established, great. You need to start focusing more on this. Shouldn't be focused, so focused on short term sales. Now, what you can do is you can reach out to these organizations, these brands, these people that have a lot of influence, that have a lot of the other hand you can do is instead of wasting time building a mailing list, you can just go buy one and then borrow credibility in your messaging from somebody else that has already established brand credibility. But one of the easiest ways to start is to use this tool called Sparke Torro. I'm just going to walk you through what this will look like. So you go to spark dot com, it's free, you get, I think, 10 searches per month, absolutely free, not trying to sell you anything.

It's just a very useful tool. And what we're going to do is we're going to say that. Our target is product managers. I don't know, maybe we're selling them productivity tools, software, maybe a chair that won't hurt your back because you're sitting down all day, something like that, something to help you get through, whatever it is. I don't care who your customer is. Maybe it's medical doctors. Maybe it's people looking for wouldn't gazebos. It could be anybody. You can find them all here on the spectrum. So we're going to say that my audience uses this word in their profile, product manager. And the great thing about the search engine is it's not searching for topics or search queries. You're searching for how the audience is defined.

And when you're doing marketing, when you're doing startup marketing, you're interested in who the target customer is, not necessarily just what search terms are out there. Because sometimes it's very easy to target people based on who they are rather than behavioral metrics, which may be a little bit more difficult to track. So what we're going to do here is we're going to find out. What brands, what people, what social channels already have credibility with these product managers that we're going to try to sell to so that we can piggyback off of them, we can email them, we can reach out to them, we can do joint marketing with them.

We can start inviting them to our channels and we can start volunteering our content to participate in their channels because it's much easier to tap into an existing audience, an existing brand, existing effluence, existing credibility than trying to start from zero. When you're not a celebrity, you're not famous and you don't have a massive following Mansbach torero. You can see the navigation here on the left. I'm looking at podcasts. Here are the podcasts. They follow rework podcasts from base camp Masters of Scale with Reid Hoffman Guy, The Kevin Ross Show and first big podcast. These are the guys that have credibility. Make friends with these people, see if you have something of value to add, to get on the reworked podcast as a guest or this podcast or this podcast or that one, I've had a lot of success doing that.

I, for example, in the veterinary industry, reached out to the most influential podcasters in the industry, had the CEO go on there as a guest and bam, suddenly you have access to this wide, receptive audience that wants to hear what you have to say. Let's take a look at YouTube channels, OK? We want to get in front of these product managers. Might be a bit hard getting in slack in base camp, a little bit too big. Five hundred startups. Maybe you can have something, a story to offer them or some research you've done. The product managers would be interested. It probably would be hard getting on the senator's channel here, but you could upgrade your account to see access to some of the smaller channels, which might be an easier way to get your foot in the door.

We can look at the press to see what press hits the product, the TechCrunch, maybe a little bit more difficult, but we could start with the VIRGE and work our way up. So some of these channels are going to be easier to get into. Some of them are going to be smaller or huge. Just play around and put them all into a cold email to message them all. You can go to their website and hit their contact us page and just offer them something of value. Often that's let's say you're a PhD and you've done a dissertation. Go on there, talk about that. Let's say that you've had a success story about your customer that was at a restaurant or whatever, and go to the restaurant influencers and write to them and say, hey, I have this great story. I'd love to go on and talk about it.

Don't don't talk about how great your product is. Just give them useful content, give them stories, and then you're going to build your own credibility in this way. So the chapteric example of doing this is to go to social media and you figure out who has credibility on Twitter. We can get Twitter stats. So this guy has or this brand product can't or nineteen thousand plus. OK, so some of these are going to be super, super high level people. But with this Ryan

Hoover guy, LinkedIn, we can see how much influence he must have, some credibility. And LinkedIn can check out his LinkedIn profile. And we can see the percentage of the audience. It's 19 percent of our product manager audience by going to our product line, maybe they have advertising options on product content. We could use that as a marketing channel.

We can see the number of social followers they have. How long would it take you to build a social following of six hundred thirty eight thousand people? It's going to take you forever. It's going to take you years. It's going to be a huge investment. Don't do that. Just leverage the followership that is already out there. You're going to be way more efficient. Portero it's just one way to find out who has credibility that you can tap into. There are other people you can partner with. So you can go to Amazon and you can just say who's written a book on product management? Reach out to that author and connect with that person on LinkedIn, on Facebook, on their website, whatever.

OK, so this guy here who we got, Jackie Bavaro and Gayle, let's right out to those people and say, hey, listen, I know you have a great audience. Here's something that I think I would love. Well, let's talk about it further. You could go to any channel, you could go to Google, you can go to Facebook. One approach I use is I go to Facebook, I find a group. So, for example, find a group of Shopify sellers, talk to the administrator of that group and say, listen, we have this product. I'd like you to do a demo of it. We're going to pay you seventy five dollars to take a look at it, give us your feedback. And then after you get that call, you could say something. Hey, are you interested in promoting this to your audience? We're going to give you a fifty percent commission on the sales, thirty percent commission, whatever. So build partnerships with people that have credibility already so you don't have to.

Approaching Influencers

I'm going to walk you through how you may want to reach out to influencers and then do that by showing you the approach that I use in the gas industry, the software industry. So once you have a list of target influencers, maybe you've got Fassbach Torro, maybe manually went through Amazon or YouTube and started compiling a database. The first approach that I would take is to offer them a perpetually free account for your product, and you might want to label this as something special, like a VIP account or an unlimited account. You can email them, you can write them on their Facebook page or whatever channel that they're on for social media. You can connect with them on LinkedIn to write to them. If you have connections, personal or professional or otherwise, you can go through that person to get a conversation started.

If the person is very high profile and they're difficult to get a hold of what you may want to try as direct mail or a handwritten letter. And another thing to note is that they may not respond right away and it doesn't necessarily mean they're not interested. You may need to follow up four more times before they respond, especially in cases where they have somebody else managing their social media, which is very often the situation. It may appear as though it's that influencer with their photo, but it's actually someone else that's managing the account. Now, there are ways to automate this, but again, don't focus on automation in the beginning with your growth, hacking just focuses on manually doing things to prove concepts and then approach the scalability factor.

So to be able to scale something like this, you use a program such as Outreach or Leme List, where you can have a whole series of follow up emails with personalization. And there are other tools you can use for things like LinkedIn. A good thing is that once you have a notable influencer who signs up for your product, you've set a precedent in a form of social proof, an authority that will entice other people to follow up. So you can send, for example, an email here where you're talking about how the other person just signed up. Why are you essentially the other thing to note is that in some cases, in my experience, it's actually been easier getting high profile people to review my product or endorse my product than getting those kinds of low level or mid-level influencers.

So don't go in with a lot of assumptions that it's going to be easier. I know from my experience when I was applying to business school, I had top schools that were more interested in me than lower ranked schools. And I don't know why, but I think that sometimes people just don't believe you when they don't think you're actually interested and they might just think it's spam or a trick or something like that. But a high profile person or a high profile school, in my case, knows that you're interested and that they're going to take you seriously. Now, the other thing is that not everybody is going to be interested in free access to your product, so in a lot of cases the influencer isn't actually the same as the customer, they're not like a prototype of the customer there. They're different.

They're an influencer that isn't sort of an industry type person. So here you may need other incentives. So, for example, free merchandise that you have to actually mail to them. A lot of people do this in the business consumer space because they want you to, for example, show off their products through t-shirts, their microphones, whatever. Another thing that you can do is pay them to do a demo, similar to what I talked about, about getting Business-to-business people to respond to offers, is just to entice them with money or gift cards. So, for example, this Visa gift card I have in the upper right. Some of the research that I saw with influencers and how they want to be compensated is they just want money. So they want to be paid a thousand dollars for a blog or a social media push, or they want to do a three thousand dollar webinar or something like that.

My bias and, you know, statistically, maybe this isn't true, but I try to avoid that. At first. You don't want to just pay for a post. What you want to do is align incentives so that that person has an added benefit of actually getting people to sign up for your product or an added benefit of them actually using the product. So you and the influencer should behave as though you're both representing the same company. Now, the thing is, an influencer who is well established and is successful is not going to want to take a pure commission style compensation structure. So the way you can configure the relationship is that you give them a guarantee. So we're going to guarantee you five thousand dollars.

But if you're able to get, I don't know, two hundred people to sign up for the product, then we're going to give you 30 percent commission or 50 percent commission, whatever it is. The other thing you can do is have a mixed compensation structure. So, hey, we're going to give you two thousand dollars. But because we want you to actually endorse the product and not just talk about it casually, like an ad that's not very convincing at all, we're going to give you an extra 10 to 15 percent of revenue for those new paying customers, something like that. You have to do the math to figure out your customer acquisition cost.

So one way I've done this before is with attribution. So I talked earlier about how you shouldn't obsess over attribution, but when you're talking about paid media spend, it can be very helpful. So one way I did it was I had people doing live chapters about I think it was 10 to 20 of them, and I gave them each a unique link. So I was able to see how many people were signing up and able to see who was generating me users for five cents versus 10 cents, that sort of thing. Another thing is that sometimes you just get free publicity and I've had that happen with Tier one influencers, so as your influencer program starts to get more advanced, you may want to build a partnership program where they get a certification badge to get a percentage of recurring revenue.

You give them marketing opportunities. You give them exclusive access to data and information and training. You give them some sort of status or, you know, something like you're a VIP user or you give them some sort of title like chief evangelist Guy Kawasaki is the chief evangelist for Caneva, something like that. Other tips is that you can just invite influencers to be a guest on your podcast, webinar or whatever. That's great, because it's going to entice more people to show up if they have a recognized brand. There you can be a guest on their podcast or they were webinar invite them to a YouTube channel. And, Of course, just make sure that you're focused on what we call the collaborative value proposition. It's what's in it for them.

Latch onto Larger Companies 1

Latch on to larger companies. This is one of the most important opportunities that marketers miss because they're so focused on the target customer that they miss target partners, collaborator's. Recognize that your target market isn't just customers, but also the partners you choose to work with. That means that choosing partners is a strategic decision, not just a small tactical consideration. One of the main reasons I recommend working with larger companies is because you need to stop doing everything from scratch. Working from scratch gives you very little leverage and it's a slow process filled with mistakes and wrong turns. You can bypass all of this by latching on to partners. A single partnership with a large company can generate more customers than 10 years worth of demand generation.

So be wise about how you spend your time. One example is to work with publishers such as Penguin in the book industry or AEA in the chapter game industry. This gives you access to larger resources and connections to make your new product a success. Why market your product yourself when you could piggyback off of larger publishers? Another example is to publish on a platform such as Chrome Webster. There are lots of successful apps on here that you may have never even heard of, but they were very successful because they latched on to an existing marketplace for apps.

Jungle Scout is one company that had a lot of success early on by promoting a chrome web store and ask yourself, am I better off selling this product on my own or optimizing it to be sold on an existing platform with a steady flow of potential buyers? Licensing your royalties is another popular approach that's used by inventors. A great book further details this called One Simple Idea, which outlines the process of buying a patent pending for your product and then soliciting potential companies to sell them the rights to use that patent pending. This gives you tremendous leverage.

Latch onto Larger Companies 2

Another angle is to work with large retailers such as Amazon or Wal-Mart, many of the most successful e-commerce companies don't actually have their own e-commerce stores. They just sell on Amazon and mastered the art of search engine optimization on Amazon, getting reviews and finding missed opportunities for new products or for retail arbitrage. Similarly, you can sell in Wal-Mart stores or on Wal-Mart.com. Getting in the big stores means you don't have to do the work of acquiring customer traffic to your own store or website. Steam is a great marketplace. If you sell chapter games, consider self publishing here. Winning a large RFP request for proposal is one way to catapult yourself to success. A single big contract with the government could generate a year's worth of revenue. The best part is that these groups are usually publicly listed for you to bid on.

You may also be solicited to respond to a large company's request for proposals. Make sure you invest a lot of time tailoring your proposals to their needs as these big contracts are well worth the effort. App stores are a great opportunity as these are relatively new compared to other platforms like Google, don't just limit yourself to Apple and Google, however, consider intuits apps dot com where you can see a number of apps that latch on to the Intuit ecosystem. Salesforce has a similar ecosystem that you can tap into. I know several highly successful software businesses. Built on selling through the Salesforce Appexchange.

One of the reasons I highly recommend selling on these platforms is because App Store optimization is usually quite easy. Search engine optimization for Google has gotten very sophisticated over the years and takes a lot of time and effort. But the search engine algorithms for these platforms are not nearly as sophisticated as Google's. So it's quite easy to show up on the first page for keywords. If you invest time in writing keyword dense titles, subtitles and body copy, or simply drumming up more reviews by soliciting your customer base, that kind of marketing doesn't cost a single cent.

Avoid Perfectionism & Take Non-Financial Risks

One of the most important keys to success with startup marketing is to avoid perfectionism. And take non financial risks. And I'm going to walk you through a few examples, so I was listening to the CEO of a company that is valued at over one hundred million between one hundred million, two hundred million dollars. And this company helps a lot of startups, a lot of small business owners. And when the CEO was asked, what do your successful customers have in common? The number one thing he pointed out is that they are not perfectionists. So all too often, what happens with. Independent business owners, start ups, CEOs, inventors, founders, if they try to create the perfect product and sometimes that takes years and years.

So, for example, book authors will spend maybe five years writing the perfect book. They release it into the market and it's just crickets. Nobody buys it. Nobody's interested because there is no market feedback along the way. And I've seen this before at startups, too, that spend millions of dollars in product development, five years perfecting something, releasing it to market, and then the product fails. This is surprisingly common, I was having a conversation recently with somebody in Armenia who's observed the same thing. I'm seeing it in the US, I'm seeing it in Canada, I've seen it with small business owners. I'm seeing it with medium business owners.

You need to recognize that perfectionism is not that valued, particularly in the early stages, because in the early stages, you don't really know what's going to be successful. So the payoff of getting something perfect is very, very small because you may be perfecting something in a direction that the market doesn't value. So it's much better in the early stages to try a bunch of things. And there are many different applications of this. So at the very tactical level, this could mean creating 20 different LinkedIn ads. And when you run ads on LinkedIn, it'll automatically, using artificial intelligence, try to optimize to figure out which ad, which campaign is performing the best to get the results you want.

You do the same thing with Facebook ads. You can do the same thing when you do cold email. If you send cold email through a tool like glumness, just create a whole bunch of cold emails, do a bunch of random lab tests and just double down on whatever works, whatever grabs, and then tweak your marketing based on actual market feedback. Do not try to get things perfect in the beginning. Now, there are a couple of key reasons for this when you're small. You can afford to be imperfect, you can afford to make a lot of mistakes because you have nothing to lose. You don't have a reputation, you don't have a lot of money, you don't have a lot of assets to lose, there's nothing for you to lose.

So you should be taking more risks now as you get larger, as you get more credibility, as you have a reputation that needs protection. That's when you need to be more conservative. That's when you need to be more perfectionistic. That's when you need to start worrying about lawsuits, because that's when companies are going to start poking holes in you, because if they do sue you and are successful, they actually have money to get. But who's going to sue somebody that doesn't have money? Who's going to sue a company that's not already successful? So the time to take risks is in the beginning and risk. What do I mean? I mean, bold marketing.

I mean creative marketing. I mean, doing things like cold emailing. I mean, doing things like talking to the CEOs of companies that you think won't respond to you. I mean, asking for a lot of money when you're not sure if you're going to get it. Try a bunch of stuff. Be agile, be experimental. Now, the time to be more careful is later on. One thing I want to point out, though, is that the risks you take in the beginning are non-financial risks. You have more time, you have more agility. You can move quicker. You can be more creative, but you don't have a lot of money. So don't spend ten thousand dollars on a PR blitz. Don't try a TV campaign for thirty thousand dollars.

I'm not talking about risks that require a lot of money. I'm talking about risks that require creativity, boldness, and unconventionalism. That's the kind of risk you should be taking. And I want to call out somebody else here, this is a Stanford business professor, Jeffrey Pfeffer. And one of the things that he points out is this. Strange psychological anomaly in the work world where employees are surprisingly risk averse. And those that recognize that there is a cost, that there's a price associated with being risk averse are the ones that can be very successful because they can make bold moves like asking for a lot more money than their peers might.

Or doing things to get attention, doing that big presentation in a company that's going to give you visibility. Another thing I want to point out is research from Harvard Business School, and there is a professor there that has written a book about the entertainment industry. It's called Blockbusters. And in that book, what she mentions is that there are celebrities who are incredibly successful and they're essentially a winner take all market, whether there was a handful of celebrities in a given entertainment industry, whether it's sports or movies or books or whatever. And they are incredibly successful, even though. Not all of their products are successful, so there are movie stars that are in very poor movies, but nobody cares, actually all that they remember is the last blockbuster that those people were in.

So the point I'm trying to get away from here is that. You can take risks, you can have duds, you can have failures, you can have ads that go nowhere. You can do things that people might cringe at. But it doesn't really matter because the things that people remember, the things that you're going to get noticed for, the things that you're going to get praised for are the things that people do notice are the things that do actually become successful. So if people are criticizing what you've done, you've done your job because you've actually gotten a lot of visibility, a lot of brand awareness. So mission accomplished. You can take a lot of risks. You can have a lot of failures because it doesn't matter, because it's that one in 10 that's extremely successful. That's all that matters.

Marketplaces 1

Something I've noticed with a lot of the successful startups that I've worked with is that they focus on marketplaces. So marketplaces, for example, are places like Amazon or eBay or digital marketplaces or perhaps Steve for chapter games. And there are a few reasons why I think startups are very successful when they do this. And I'm going to go into more detail in a second. But I think one of the most important things is that on a marketplace is people that actually have purchase intent. So when you do something like a cold email or an advertising campaign on Facebook. Or you create a blog that has a lot of very valuable, interesting content.

You may get a lot of interest from people. In terms of consuming the content, they don't necessarily have purchase intent, but when you focus on marketplaces, despite the fact that you're up against a lot of competition, you're actually gaining access to a receptive audience of people that are actively looking to buy something. And there's a big difference between somebody that is simply interested in reading a blog post or an e-book and somebody that's actually interested in making a purchase. Now, we also find this with Google. People are actively looking for solutions, but it's actually much easier to get access to buyers through marketplaces. And I'll talk about why that's the case in a moment.

Now, one of the reasons that startups should be focusing on the marketplace is perhaps more than they should, based on this screenshot here that I've gotten from the Business to Business Institute from LinkedIn. Now, this is specifically about business to business sellers, but it could also apply to consumer sellers. And basically what we're seeing here is that in the beginning, when you're first starting your company and as you're growing it, you want to focus on market buyers. So these are people that are actively looking to make a purchase. Later on, once you're larger and more successful, you want to focus on out of market buyers.

So these are people that could potentially have a need for what you're selling in the future, but they're not actively looking for it. And one of the easiest ways to hit these in market buyers, these bottom of funnel people, is by going to the marketplaces where they're shopping. Now, one thing that you might be surprised by here is you actually focus on the top of a funnel as you get larger. And in the beginning, you focus on the bottom of everything. This is counterintuitive because a lot of the marketing advice out there suggests that you should start at the top of the funnel and work your way down.

I completely agree with the BTB Institute on this, I also agree with Salesforce on this, which is that the focus should really be on the bottom of the funnel initially. And then as you're successful, as you grow a business, then you start moving up the funnel to get the out of market buyers, the people that are further away from actually making a purchase decision. And that may surprise you, you may hear a lot of marketing gurus out there say, no, no, you need to start at the top of the funnel, no focus on the people that are actually going to pay you, then worry about the people that could potentially pay you in the future. OK, so one of the reasons that it's easier to perform well on marketplaces compared to other channels such as Google, for example, is because Asso or App Store optimization is incredibly easy.

Now, I'm not saying that that's true of all marketplaces, but I would say as a general rule of thumb, it is easier to optimize for searches on app stores or marketplaces in general than it is to optimize for search engines through Google, through Bing, etc.. The reason is because

Google has optimized their algorithm for search over a long period of time and it's become very sophisticated. So it's no longer a matter of just keyword stuffing or getting as many backlinks as possible. So it used to be very simple to rank highly on Google for search engines and you could effectively game the system. You could embed your website with a bunch of keywords and then just make the keywords.

Waitz you can't even see them. And that's how you got to the top of Google, but you can't do that anymore. That's considered black hat techniques. Back in the day, we didn't even have that term that it was a black hat technique. We were just experimenting and seeing what worked. And then they started penalizing people for doing those sorts of things, those kinds of hacks. But what we're seeing on app stores and marketplaces is that. Ranking highly is very simple, the algorithms are rudimentary there where Google was maybe 10 years ago. So it's simply a matter of putting keywords into the title of your listing. It's just getting more reviews on your listing.

It's just putting some keywords, keyword density into your description. So it's not that hard. I've done App Store optimization, marketplace optimization, where I'm able to get results within like three minutes. I can get to the first page of search results within a few minutes. You can't do that with Google anymore. I mean, it can take three months to get to the top Google or longer, depending on how competitive your space is. So by focusing on marketplaces, you're able to quickly get access to a receptive audience of people that are actively looking for a solution. And despite the fact that there's competition, the algorithms that are driving marketing visibility are very simple.

And you can do something like just send an email to your existing customers, incentivizing them to write a review on your listing and that alone could substantially boost the amount of traffic that you're getting from active buyers. So let's walk through a few examples of what the marketplace might be. So I've worked in the chapter game industry and I've seen how successful steam can be.

Marketplaces 2

So let's think about why a chapter game may be more successful on Steam than trying to sell it on your own website. Well, the people that buy chapter games are established and familiar with steam. They trust the brand. They are familiar with the process. And if you're trying to get somebody to download an X file or something that could be malicious, are you more likely to do that through a channel that you trust or channel you don't trust? Well, Of course, you're going to do it through a trust, a channel. There are other key benefits, too, like the fact that people are actually going to steam actively looking for chapter games or browsing, they're looking for things to buy, and they don't necessarily know that your brand exists. They don't know that your chapter game exists, but they might stumble across it.

If you're in the right category, if you're promoting yourself actively there, you're going to get a receptive audience. Now, when I worked at PlayStation, we had multimillion dollar television campaigns that are designed to create awareness for new chapter game brands. And with that kind of budget and with the trust of PlayStation tagged on to those games, I was able to be quite successful with generating sales. But you don't have that kind of budget as a startup. You can't do a massive awareness campaign. So your tactics with regard to marketing are going to be fundamentally different.

It's going to be more about gaining visibility within marketplaces like steam. So another thing that we noticed is that with these smaller indie games, often what they do is they provide something that large chapter games used to do, which was the demos. You have a demo experience to try out the product. And with that kind of long tail, when we're dealing with these indie games that have small markets, you're going to see a lot more of those demo experiences. So being successful as a startup in the chapter game space looks very different than it does when you're launching a potential blockbuster through a large company like PlayStation or Xbox, whatever.

Another example is Amazon, so I've mentioned elsewhere in this Book that I've done tons of research, quantitative research, looking at successful e-commerce sellers and some of the most successful ones that get to that midsize are selling on Amazon. It's a receptive audience of paying customers. So if you're focused on Amazon, it's very hard to get distracted. You're not going to get distracted by marketing. That's fun and creative. You're going to focus on marketing that actually generates sales. And it also forces you to think in terms of competitive context. You can't be successful on Amazon if you don't have something that has superior value or vastly superior marketing because it's a competitive place.

So it forces you to hone and focus on where you're actually able to generate a profit. And one of the things that startups frequently do, founders, when they pitch venture capitalists, is they underestimate the competition. They devalue the competition. They don't realize how strong the competition is. But when you're in a competitive marketplace, you're forced to do that and you're forced to make changes quickly because you recognize the power of competition. Another example is selling an app through the Clover app marketplace. So if you have some sort of peak point of sale integration and a lot of your customers are using something like Clover, you should be on their app marketplace.

Often when you're selling software, there's usually one piece of software that is kind of the key software that your customers use. It's their CRM or their accounting system or your point of sale or their practice management system. So if you're if that fits you, if you're in the software space, then you want to latch on to that main piece of software that owns the customer relationship and sometimes is the post. If you're selling something creative like necklaces or crafts, go on Etsy. If you're trying to acquire users and traffic from the get go from Ground Zero, it's going to be very expensive. It's going to be very time consuming. You don't want to have to do that if you go to Etsy.

Etsy has already invested a lot of time, a lot of money building an audience of recurring traffic of people that are interested in the kinds of things that they're interested in Bede's or interested in jewels. They're interested in handcrafted things. Why build that audience yourself? Just tap into the existing audience that Etsy has already built for you? Yes, it's competitive. Yes. You're going to be up against other artists, but who cares? That's where the money is, you got to go where the money is, even if there's a competition app dotcom is one of cookbook's marketplaces. They also have a desktop marketplace as well. But listings on both. This is a place you can go if your users are using quick bucks and you sell a quick book integration.

There's no need to go and build a massive audience, quick book users, they're already captive looking for apps to install. You can do that on the app. You saw Books you create interesting educational content just to go to. That's where the people are that want to consume and pay for that kind of content. Ali Express. People looking for interesting items from China, perhaps they can't find it on Amazon, they can't find it on eBay. Go on, Ali Express. People are going to trust it. They're going to be willing to and their credit card information there because they're familiar with AliExpress. You don't have to build that. Trust yourself. You want to gain access to Fortune 500 companies that are using Salesforce.

Go on the Salesforce app exchange. I've heard of this one company a few years ago, built a multimillion dollar business and all they're doing is tapping into the Salesforce ecosystem. They're just a little. A little I don't want to see him, just a small player in the sales force world that's able to build a very successful startup around that ecosystem, you don't need to be the next sales force. You can just be a little tacky on that ecosystem. And that can be a very viable business for you as a startup. Few other examples that we look at international markets. You can join Torkel. So I've lived in Indonesia where people talk about PDA. They also use Sharpie Lozada. I've never heard of this one, but maybe you have eBay. Perhaps you're in the business of buying and selling used items or new items.

And eBay is the kind of receptive audience that you want to tap into. Other examples are places like Airbnb, any sort of matchmaking service. You can try to build a brand for your rental units. You can try to build a brand for your own breakfast in bed. But why do that? Why bother? You can just go on the Airbnb listing. It's going to focus your marketing on what's able to generate sales. And that's going to be things like nice photos, nice listing descriptions, getting positive reviews instead of getting distracted by this fun stuff like how do we build a brand? How do we do some creative marketing? Let's just focus on what people are actually willing to pay for. And by going on a listing like Airbnb, that's going to compel you to do that.

ASO 1 - Keyword Research

Next, I'm going to talk about App Store and marketplace optimization. You might use different words for this Asso App Store optimization or SEO search engine optimization. Usually when we talk about SEO, we're talking about Google and Bay, but search engines don't just exist on Google and Bing. They exist in marketplaces where you use search. They exist in app stores where you do search. So you could also call it search engine optimization. Now, the first question you might have is how is this growth hacking? Isn't this just ordinary digital marketing? Well, I would say that when you're optimizing for Google and Bing search results, you're doing ordinary marketing. It's slow.

It's a competitive market. And it is something that builds up over time. But when you're dealing with app stores and marketplaces, often what you find is that even sophisticated, well-funded companies have not put a lot of time into keyword research, into making sure they have enough reviews to get to the top of the listings. So often what these are is low supply markets where you can get results very quickly. Now, in some of my experience, optimizing listings in app stores, I'm actually able to get to the front page in a matter of minutes, literally minutes, not months, not weeks, not days, but within minutes of making some small tactical changes, I'm able to get there. So in that sense, I would definitely call this a form of growth hacking.

One thing to point out is that it's much easier than Google or Bing, the algorithms that are typically used on app stores and in marketplaces. And again, I'm talking a lot at the Times about very sophisticated companies like Intuit. Sophisticated companies, but the algorithms that they use for research are not that sophisticated, they're where Google was maybe 10 years ago, and if you were doing marketing back then, you would realize that optimizing for AltaVista, optimizing for Google, optimizing for Yahoo! Was much easier. There were techniques, hacks that you could do to get to the front page very easily. You can't do that anymore.

The other algorithms are too sophisticated and there's also just too much competition. Too many people invest it in search engine optimization. But that's not the case with app stores to a large extent. But there are also some disadvantages, so you can get results faster, it's much more simplistic to get results. But the other thing is that it's less established and because it's less established, it makes certain research more difficult. And the primary case here is keyword research. You don't have data, for example, on how many people are searching for a given key word on apps, dot com. You don't have data for how many people are searching for a given keyword on steam. So it's kind of like the Wild West. You're entering new territory.

There aren't set rules. This is the kind of place where a growth hack or an entrepreneurial, agile person is able to play around with different tactics and see what works. And the great thing is that because you can get results quickly, it's easy to get feedback so that you can make adjustments. So I'm going to walk you through a few examples of how to do keyword research, and the first set of examples is really about the autocomplete function. So because we don't have a keyword research plan or in a lot of cases, especially with these smaller marketplaces, what you're going to do is start typing in a word that's relevant to what you're selling. So here I'm typing in something I envy. Maybe that's inverse invoicing that I'm selling. Maybe it's inventory.

And what's going to happen here on the Salesforce app exchange is it's going to give me a list of keywords that people search for. And what I would do is I would start creating a spreadsheet and list these keywords as potential keywords for me to optimize for. And then what you can do is you can actually do a search for that keyword. So I might hit enter after hitting inventory management and just look at things like how many reviews are there? Is this a popular app? So you can start making guesses in terms of the volume of people that you think intuitively are searching for that keyword. And there's going to be a lot of guesswork. Again, it's like the Wild West.

You do the same thing on Amazon with Amazon, you probably want to specify the specific category or store. So if you're selling books, you can select the Kindle store or you can select books as a category. I typed in investing here and you can see Investing for Dummies, Investing Keynes, investing for beginners, investing in real estate. So here I'm saying seeing where the demand is in terms of search engine keywords. And what you might decide, for example, investing for kids, maybe that becomes the title of your book, maybe originally when you wrote the book, it was simple Investing for Dummies. Well, when I look at these keywords, all right, I'm just going to change the title on Amazon and you can even change it after you publish it.

Now we're going to go into the category of appliances, so I have a friend who's interested in getting it in the microwave space, so he's thinking about ordering microwaves from China through Alibaba, selling them. So maybe he wants to set up a store on Amazon. Well, let's do some keyword research. A case where a microwave countertop, microwave and toaster oven combo microwave over the range. OK, so none of these keywords is actually relevant to the specific use case of why he wanted to sell a specific microwave. So that has a number of implications. One is maybe it's just not a viable product offering because there's not enough demand.

The other is that he just needs to start going after other keywords because people aren't actively searching for it, even if they do want it. Express, just like Amazon, starts typing in the word and you're going to see a list of what people are actually searching for, which is a proxy for how much demand there is for that keyword. Audible, which is a fairly new frontier, not as established as Kindle, more established perhaps than other audio based platforms that are starting to come out right now. And we can use the autocomplete function here. So I typed in and and we have anxious people, Animal Farm and weird anxiety. So there's a mix of keywords. There's also a mix of authors and titles Of course. That's the same thing if you're in this new neck, necklaces for women, necklaces, necklaces with names.

So you may decide, hey, you know what? I have this necklace I'm going to sell. Why don't we make it specifically as a necklace is for mom and then use that keyword in the positioning, perhaps create a separate listing that's catered to necklaces for women to see. Can I go after a broader market or do I have to teach down? The mobile app stores are also a good place to start doing keyword research with autocomplete, I went into Google Play, I typed in Monkey and you can see monkey games, Monkey City monkey. Steam, a marketplace for chapter games in this case, what you're going to find is that there really isn't autocomplete. What they offer instead is a population of products that start with R when I type in R, so here the R stands for Rainbow six. This is for rebirth.

So they're just giving you product selection. They're not giving you keywords. So in cases like that, it becomes actually even more difficult to do keyword optimization because there is no autocomplete to give you inspiration for keywords. Now, the good thing is that if you are in a marketplace that is fairly large, has a lot of volume, but the downside is that those tend to be more competitive markets. You can use special tools. So, for example, if you were selling a book on Amazon, you could use a tool like Publisher Rocket, which I tried out myself, and they were going to give you data so that you don't just need to rely on autocomplete keywords.

So this shows you what keyword shoppers type into Amazon and see the list keywords here, number of competitors, average monthly earnings to see. Is that a high demand market you want to participate in? They're also giving you Google searches, sometimes estimated Amazon searches per month. So how many shoppers search for that keyword and then a competitive scope? So how competitive is this keyword? Another tool that you could use is Selex, which is going to give you keyword data for optimizing your Amazon listing, which may not necessarily be a book. It could be glove's, for example, demonstrated here. And what they do is they have a keyword and then they show you the search volume for that keyword. You can see that work at Glove's is really where the high demand is for that.

Now, another thing I want to point out is there are lots of these tools out there for keyword optimization on different platforms. The thing is, again, you're in the Wild West. A lot of these are not going to be perfect. They're going to use flawed algorithms, they're going to try to approximate demand, there are going to be things that are going to skew averages. So, for example, there's a book I'm interested in that's three hundred dollars and they're going to be people that are giving away products for free. So there's a lot of data in there that is going to skew the averages. And you might get a distorted perspective on how much products sell, how much volume there is for keywords.

So you really need to test these out and find the one that's most effective for you. The other thing is that we're going to be tools out there that are a little more general. So, for example, there were keyword research tools for Amazon, but they're not going to be particularly effective if you're selling a book on Amazon. Now, they're going to be fine for selling appliances and toys and kind of the prototypically use case for Amazon. But you're going to want to down and use a tool that specific books, if that's the case that you're in. So some of these are not going to be reliable. I recommend trying out a few of them. They're going to have a free trial. Some of them are completely free. So this particular one keyword tool is completely free, but sometimes it's questionable.

Is the data coming in from this good or not? And you can see that they're actually providing data for different platforms. So there's Google, which you can use keyword planner for anyways. YouTube being Amazon, eBay, play store, Instagram, Twitter. So that's great. They're giving you a lot of options for free. It's a good place to start because it's free. And here, comparing what I did earlier with Amazon, you can put in some of those keywords here and it'll give me an estimate for search volume and show me the trend. Is this a growing market or not? The cost per click and the competition, which you can see is high. So my friend who wants to enter the microwave market should be aware that you're going to have some competition in organic search in that space.

Now, another example is when you're selling a mobile app, you can use a tool like this one, and what it's going to do is provide you with a traffic estimate, iPhone difficulty, iPad difficulty or so something like sensor tower can be effective if you're focused on mobile app stores. Similarly, you can use a product like App Annie, which I've used before when I was in charge of marketing for a mobile app, the mobile app version of another product, and they're going to give you information like search volume difficulty. And what you can do is you can actually combine this data with data that you're getting from another tool like sensor tower and then see which one is the most reliable with the use case that is specific to you.

ASO 2 - Optimization

Once you have a set of target keywords that you want to optimize for, the next step is to start experimenting with the listing optimization. Now, something I want to point out here is that it may not necessarily be straightforward how you optimize for the marketplace or whatever store that you're participating in. So it kind of depends on how established it is and whether there are enough suppliers on that market for there to be a set of rules that people have discovered in terms of what optimizes your listing. Now, if you're on one of those established marketplaces like Amazon or Google Play, you can just Google to find out what those elements are. So they're going to be key things like the title, the subtitle, and HTML information.

But what I'm going to provide for you is a kind of a framework for looking at app listings in general and looking for patterns in terms of what may be driving the performance in terms of getting to the top of search results. So here, for example, I'm looking at Stockholm, which is one of the main marketplaces for it, and what I've done is I've selected the category to calculate quotes. So instead of doing a search, I just went into this category and there are lists of different apps here. So one of the things that stands out most to me is that the number one app in the listing simply has the most amount of reviews and not by a small margin. Look at this. One, almost two thousand reviews, second place only 50, so the number of reviews is often a strong driver of where your ranking is in App Store optimization, and there are different ways that you can get more reviews. And one of the easiest ones is to simply identify who you're most satisfied with.

Customers are using your net promoter score, using just feedback from the customer success managers looking at behavior. So somebody that's using it more frequently is probably more satisfied with it and just prompting them in your app or if you're selling a physical product, maybe you could email them or give them a call and just say, hey, we'd love to have you write a review. And you have to comply with rules here, so some marketplaces will say you can't actually ask people to write a positive review, but maybe you can incentivize them to write an honest review so you don't want to get kicked off the marketplace. OK, I did another search here for construction. And as you can see, the first ranking is the one with the most amount of reviews and it's by a wide margin.

So the first is three hundred eighteen reviews, second only forty six. Reviews of the thing that stands out here is that the little write up that's below the name of the app or below the title often has the word construction. So if we look at the top ones here, even this one has construction as well. So I did another search for a restaurant. And what we can see here is that the one with the most amount of reviews, seventeen's just one more than second place is still the first ranking and restaurant is showing up in the. Second text like the subtitle here in most of these cases now, the other thing that stands out here is this one, which only has only six reviews, has restaurant or restaurants, the plural form in the actual title.

So that suggests that perhaps you get a bonus by having the restaurant, the key word in the title itself rather than just the subtitle. And that may compensate for the fact that you have fewer reviews. The other thing that would be a good hypothesis is that having the keyword earlier helps. So for example, the first place ranking, we see restaurant as the first word, whereas here it's actually the third word. Now, I don't know for a fact that that's true, but that's something you can experiment with, putting keywords further to the left, putting keywords in the title instead of the subtitle and the number of reviews. I went to the Amazon Kindle store and I did a search for a sales funnel, and here's the interesting thing. We have two books, they're both bestsellers now.

The second book here has a sales funnel actually in the title, and the second book has more reviews. So this raises the question, why is this book ranking above this book? Now, it could just be that it's random testing. So sometimes Amazon might decide, oh, we're going to randomly give another product a chance, putting it above it, and we'll just see if it gets more sales or not so that that could be happening. But there's probably more to the picture here. And let's dive a little bit deeper. So one of the key things here is that this dotcom secrets book actually has the keyword sales funnel everywhere. It's in the title, it's in a ton of reviews.

In fact, there's an entire review chapter that you can click that says contains the category of sales funnel. So it's been stuffed with that keyword. So it's a bit of a mystery as to why this one is showing up above that one. So one of the first things is looking at the HTML. So I just clicked when I was in the chapter for this book and I viewed the source. So I looked at the actual email. And there is where you're starting to see the word funnel. Now, if you just look at the front end of this book, there's very little talking about funnels. I think I found one review mentioning funnel, but when you look at HTML, then you start seeing it everywhere. So that suggests that if you want your Amazon book to rank higher for a given keyword, you need to optimize where you can use HTML metadata.

OK, now the second factor here is that Amazon wants to make money and they're going to prioritize products that are more likely to make money. So your listing optimization is not just about can I stuff it full of keywords? That may be your first consideration, because if you don't have nobody seeing your product, there's no chance they're going to buy it. But the other key thing is just are you actually getting conversions and are you doing good copywriting that's actually going to generate a sale, which is the art of marketing in terms of doing sales like these. And if we look at the titles, they sell like crazy or dotcom secrets. I don't know about you, but my subjective opinion is that this is a much more compelling benefit than this one. It's very clear what the promises here you were going to sell like crazy are going to make a ton of money.

So when I see a book like that, I'm going to buy it. When I see a book that says dotcom secrets, I don't know what the benefit is there, there's no clear promise. And not only is there no clear promise, but there's no clear North Star in terms of what that promise is here. It sells like crazy, right? There's a descriptor there. It's not just selling a lot. There's an emotional appeal there and there's a bit of excitement that gets built. No offense to dotcom secrets doing very well. Top seller. I just think from a sales perspective, conversion perspective, there's a reason that this is probably doing better, even though they've probably done a better job seeding reviews here, which is probably the reason that they have more reviews.

OK, if we go to mobile app stores, we can do a similar assessment and just form some hypotheses and test them. So, for example, I did a search here for a timesheet and we can see that almost all of the top listings have a timesheet in the actual app title. In this case, they're not spacing out those two words, but that's fine. I guess the algorithms are sophisticated enough to recognize what I'm talking about. And then I'm sure that they're going to have a timesheet in the description and perhaps in the HTML data as well. Did another search here for a calorie counter and my fitness pal showed up at number one. And almost all of these have a calorie counter in the actual title. So you can see that there's a pattern across app stores where you really need to put keywords in your title.

Don't get committed to a keyword too early because you may find when you actually go to market on an App Store marketplace that you've got to change it because that's where the demand is. That's what people are actually searching for. OK, now if we take a closer look at my fitness pal will notice that they don't actually have a keyword, a calorie counter a lot in there or right up other than seeing it here in the title. But where you do start to see it is in one case and one review here. So that could be a driver of their search engine optimization. I'm a bit skeptical because I only saw one review that had it, but where I definitely see it is in the HTML. And this is kind of the back end that a lot of people don't realize when they're doing something like App Store optimization is focusing on the HTML data.

Be Specific

One of the single most important pieces of advice I have for you with your startup marketing is to stop being vague, stop being general, start being more concrete and start being more specific. So let's walk through a few examples of what I mean by this. A lot of people, when they approach marketing, they start off with personas, so, for example, they say that the person that we want to buy our product is Hank the Hunter, or it's Froogle Farra, who's this? Twenty six year old female from Spain. The problem is that these aren't specific, these are conceptual ideas of what the people in the market might look like, and often we have a lot of stereotypes.

We have a lot of misunderstandings. And often when we do this kind of generic personal work, we're working with variables that don't really matter and don't apply to our products. So, for example, Farra here doesn't matter that she's a woman, is that even relevant to what we're selling? Sure. It's going to be relevant if you're selling something like lingerie or cosmetics. But for most of the products out there, your sex doesn't really play into whether you would buy one product or another except with consumer products. So instead, what I like to do is instead of talking in terms of these vague, generic ideas of what people are, I go and I find exactly the people that I want to buy the product. I buy a list or I build the list or I find the right targeting in the advertising platform.

So, for example, here I'm showing you what that prospect list might look like in Excel or in Google Sheets and whatever you're using. And you could pay somebody on Fiverr or on up work to compile a list for you. And now I know, OK, it's not Froogle far I'm going after. It's Sarah MacLaren, who's the director of sales at a company of five million to 10 million. All right. So now that I have a very specific idea of who I want, I can try to sell to this person. And then what's going to happen is I'm going to run into all these barriers trying to sell to this person, and then I can address the specific barriers, those specific objections that Sarah McLaren has.

So I'm moving out of the world of ideals and concepts and what I think the market looks like and into the actual market where I'm going to get real feedback, I'm going to get tons of rejection, and then I need to adjust my marketing accordingly so that I get real world results instead of conceptual results. So one of the traps that marketers fall into is they like to think in terms of high level, top of funnel, broad awareness, big market ideas. But when you're a startup, you don't need huge, big concepts to get results. You're really more focused on, OK, how do we just get these sales? Because the reality is that when you're small, when you're a startup, you don't need that many sales to become viable to grow.

And it's really at the granular level, at the specific level where we start getting results. Now, once you start to enter that kind of medium, large business, then you need to start thinking in terms of bigger, broader, maybe less specific, more conceptual. But at this stage, it's more about the concrete. It's more about how do I get Sarah McClaren to actually buy my product? And the beauty of getting more specific with your targeting is now you're going to get very specific objections that people have. People are going to say, I don't want to buy your product because I'm using X and you don't work with X or I don't want to buy your product because Company B does it better or Company B is cheaper.

They're going to give you all these objections. It may even be just poor reviews of your products. Well, you know, I was interested in your product, but I see you have three star reviews because of X, Y and Z or your product doesn't work in my country or. No, I don't want to pay this because I would just do that. Why would I pay for your subscription to solve this problem when I can just pay somebody five dollars an hour in the Philippines to do it? So do you see what I mean? Do you see how being more specific means you're going to get specific objections for why people aren't using your product or buying it? And then one by one, you can start dismantling those arguments in your marketing so that your marketing is reacting to market feedback rather than just being some sort of idea that you canvassed out to the world.

OK, so, for example, often what I see with startups when I look at their websites is they have these high level benefits that comprise the headlines of their landing pages. It'll be something like saving you time and money. But that's so vague and it's so undifferentiated from what the other startups are communicating that I just don't believe it, I don't if you're not giving me concrete specific information, I don't actually believe you can deliver on that promise. So something that would be better is saves you ten thousand dollars in electrical cost per year compared to competitors. Which are you more likely to believe? You're more likely to believe the specific case with the specific numbers compared to the specific competitor, because it's it's easier for somebody to go from a conceptual idea to concrete action, i.e.

buying your product if they can see concrete results. So that's why one of the most important things in the early stages of a startup is to build up case studies. So there's been research to show that case studies are the single most important pieces of content marketing. Now, what a lot of people do when they approach content marketing as they come up with really high level thought leadership, broad market conceptual ideas and theories. But really, if you're talking about getting sales, you're talking about getting specific results, convincing specific people to buy your product. What you want to do is sell specific outcomes. And the easiest way to do that is with case studies. And if you don't have case studies come up with theoretical scenarios, you can come up with stories.

I'm not talking about lying. I'm just saying. Present a scenario that is obviously fabricated, that shows how somebody can become transformed by buying your product, and that effectively is what a case study is and it shows it in a very specific way. So, for example, there's the book, Rich Dad, Poor Dad, and it's all built around this kind of fabricated story about a rich dad and a poor dad. And the rich dad has this attitude towards money poured in and has this attitude towards money. Was there actually a rich dad or a poor dad? I don't think so, but it communicated the message with a specific storytelling element to it, which is something that you can build into your startup marketing. Now, one of one of the most common issues I see with startup marketing is that they're not specific enough and they don't make bold decisions.

So because you don't know what people value most about your product, there's a tendency to want to fit everything in. So what ends up happening is you get this long list of benefits, long list of features, long lists of use cases, and then basically you get dismissed by customers because they're just like, oh, this is just some general smorgasbord of stuff. Instead, it's better to be specific and identify that one use case for your product or the one main benefit that really matters in the way you do that is typically you just talk to people that are in your target customer group. So, for example, you might ask on Quora, hey, people that work in operations, what do you think of kiosks or what do you think of this new lubricant? Or for consumers, you might say, why is it that men don't wear tall boots and then people are going to give you their objections? They're like, oh, well, they're too feminine or this and that or they're too inconvenient.

So what you're able to do is kind of hone in on what it is that people actually value. And another way to do it is to quantify each of the benefits. So, for example, let's say you have finance software and it saves money. It helps increase your profits. It helps you invest better. It does all sorts of things. Well, what's the one thing that actually saves the most time or makes the most money? Maybe what you realize is that actually it's the investment part of your product that matters. The rest is just kind of nice to have. It's not really something you need to focus on. And if you specify that that use case is promoted in your marketing, you're going to get a much stronger positive reaction from the market.

Because when you just throw out a list of stuff, what it shows is you don't actually understand the customers. You think that they value everything that you're presenting. But what you're actually doing is underestimating the competitors. You're underestimating the other solutions they already have in place. And that's a very common mistake people make with startup marketing. They believe their product is more valuable than it actually is. And they believe that everything that they're offering has more value than it actually does. In reality, there's probably a narrow use case where your product adds more value and you can build on that rather than trying to be this kind of all in one solution.

So related to this idea that you need to be more specific is that I want you when you're in startup marketing mode to focus on sales rather than distractions, a lot of marketing is distractions. Now, don't get me wrong, I've worked at large companies. I know what it's like to focus on marketing at that scale when you're spending millions of dollars. And I know that it's profitable. But what I'm saying is that when you're in startup mode, don't get distracted by the fun. Don't get distracted by the hype. You need to focus on sales. But here's the beauty of focusing on sales. Often it doesn't require a lot of money and it doesn't require a lot of time because sales marketing is sometimes just a short email. It's just writing and sending an email. You don't need a fancy logo. You don't need a fancy website.

You don't need a huge community. You don't need a big brand. You don't need fancy technology. It's just providing value to somebody that is willing to pay for that value. And if you need to do it manually by talking to them, by chatting with them, by getting them on the phone, you can do that and you can do all of that without this huge marketing infrastructure, without a huge design department, because really that's what you're doing in startup mode. Marketing is mostly about sales. Later on, we start transitioning to something that is different and a wider scale concept of what marketing is. So some of these distractions that I see is building awareness. Let's do some awareness marketing campaigns.

Let's build these fancy chapters. And, yeah, there is a place for that and a lot of cases. But in general, you may be more likely to get a sale if you just do something like a direct response ad or putting a listing on a marketplace to get somebody to buy your product. Or just sending out a cold email and you're going to realize that there are certain reasons people aren't buying your product and it's not because of awareness but because you haven't addressed certain objections people have. OK, another thing I see is people get excited. We're going to build a community. We're going to build this awesome interactive place where everybody is going to talk about this topic that we're in. And I'm like, that's great. That's great.

If you're in it for the long haul and you expect your company to be around for ten years, but generally in startup mode, show me the money. Show me the people that are actually going to buy the product rather than just talk. We're not interested in getting people to talk. We're interested in getting people to pay. And I'm not saying that because we're trying to be greedy. I'm saying that because we need to figure out how we create value and get people to pay for value. And then once we've done that and we've been successful at repeating that, then we can start branching into the periphery where we're building communities and audiences and whatnot. OK, another thing is branding. A lot of people think they need to build brands. Yes, in a lot of industries, that's very much true.

OK, you're selling a consumer packaged good, a fast moving consumer good. You need to build a brand because it is super competitive out there in the brand. Creates a lot of value. It creates a lot of the psychological value in your product. But in most cases that's not true. In most cases in the startup world, you need to create value that goes well beyond the brand. OK, your value is solving a specific problem. It's saving X amount of money, it's making X amount of money, it's connecting A and B, you A brand can help you with communicating that value, but it shouldn't in most cases be that important. The other issue with branding is that you get locked into a specific brand and a specific brand position that is difficult and expensive to change once you've set it up.

So it's more important to be agile and adjustable in the beginning until you kind of have a clear focus on how you create value, then you can start building a brand around that. OK, related to branding is the idea of design. OK, let's make the best looking UI, let's get the perfect and let's get a nice font. Let's get a great logo. That's fun. And it looks cool and it makes you seem credible, but it's not what sells. OK, getting sales is not about design. It's about providing value at a price that people are willing to pay for it. And that's the hard part. The hard part is thinking and understanding what the customer values and delivering value. It's not packaged in a cute design. Yes, a nice design is going to make it easier to sell. It's going to make you seem more credible and in some cases designs critical to what you're selling. Right.

If you're selling a UI, then you need to have an excellent user interface. But for most products, not really true, at least in the early stages. Design is not is not what is going to sell your product. It's going to be that use case. It's going to be the problem that you solve. It's going to be that value that you deliver. OK, and lastly here, another big distraction is technology. So part of the reason for this is that a lot of the people that dominate the conversations in the marketing world are technology companies, and a lot of them are marketing technology companies. So when you're looking at blog articles on marketing and solving this problem, not that problem. It's going to be people like Marketo that are talking about it, like HubSpot, like people that are just cranking out blog posts.

But that doesn't mean it's the solution. Don't be tricked into the Segway if I need to solve this problem so I need technology to solve this problem. Technology is great when you need to automate and you need to scale. But let me tell you, in the early stages of a startup, even in the mid stages. You don't need scalability often. It's better and easier to get labor to do what you need to do because labor is cheap in certain countries and you don't need automation to do tedious tasks. What you need is the ability to change quickly based on market reactions. Technology is not going to give you that. You're going to be locked into a software that is going to cause you all sorts of problems. So I'll just give you an example.

HubSpot is a great company, great product use, it now wasn't such a great product. Years ago when they were soliciting me to buy and I was excited. I almost thought I needed HubSpot. I couldn't believe that their marketing psychology was so brilliant they were persuading me to buy this. Like all inbound marketing is the secret.

You're going to get tons of leads, you're going to do this, that and the other thing. But then I realized that even if I had HubSpot at the time as the limited product that it was. The real bottleneck to marketing was not the technology, it was all the content that I still needed to create. So HubSpot wasn't going to solve that for me at all. It still meant that I needed to crank out a ton of white papers, a ton of blog posts, a ton of information that the market was going to consume. That was the expensive part.

Blog posts alone might cost you five hundred dollars to get a copywriter to do it. I mean, you can do it for free, but how many hours are you wasting doing that? So you see, technology was not the answer there. The answer there was content production and there's an easier route to content production, the technology, and that is hiring writers to do it for you and figuring out the specific content that's going to make the kind of impact that you need. So don't get distracted by these things. Focus on what the bottlenecks are in your sales pipeline and actually getting people to pay for your product. And you're going to get much more concrete results for startup.

Startup Marketing Methods

Welcome to the Book for startups. It can be as simple as just getting started with an email. Now, I'm going to give you another example where it's slightly more complicated to do the PR, but it's really not that much to do. So what I was doing was I was leading the marketing for Google Accelerator startup and we were marketing software dictation software for veterinarians, veterinarian clinics, etcetera. Now, the way that I approach the marketing for this company is, Why don't we find out who has the most influence among veterinarians and we'll do our marketing through them. So I went to this tool called Sparktoro, which was started by the same person that started SEOmoz, which was later rebranded as Moz, which you may be familiar with.

And I put in here my audience uses these words in their profile veterinarian and then it spits out a list of publications, influencers, brands, YouTubers, podcasts, etcetera, that are very influential around veterinarians. So, for example, podcasts was a strong focus, and that was a micro campaign that I ran, reaching out to the people that were the hosts on podcasts for veterinarians, and you can see that this particular one, according to Sparktoro, influences about 20% of the audience. So that's pretty sizable. Okay, so what did I do? I offered the top influencers, in this case, the top podcast owners, but we're also talking about people that run blogs, that publish books, all different types of media and said, We're going to give you a perpetual VIP account for the software.

And because a lot of these influencers are veterinarians, they're going to find that useful. And because they're podcasters, they're also going to find it useful because any sort of audio related equipment is going to be useful for them. So dictation software in this case and also a microphone. So giving them a perpetually free account, also giving them a white glove training experience where we get on with them on a live call to demonstrate how to use the software or how to use the hardware, etcetera. And for select people that had a lot of clout, we even mailed them a dictation microphone, a high end Philips microphone to make sure they had the best possible experience using the software.

And so not only did we raise our awareness among the people that have the most influence with veterinarians, but the next thing that we did was we were able to become podcast guests on their podcast. So that gives us a lot of reach. That gives us a lot of publicity. So this is a very simple approach to PR. It's not something overwhelming where you need to get all worked up about an interview on a news channel or getting a perfect press release or anything complicated like that. It's basically just sending emails or in some cases an Instagram message, a Facebook message, etcetera, some giving away some stuff for free and then offering to provide free content for their channel.

And this was a very successful PR campaign that ran for Google accelerator startup. So one of the key chapters from this case study on PR is that it's easier to borrow an established audience, an established influence, than it is to start from scratch. So when you're a startup, you don't have a lot of brand recognition, you don't have a lot of clout, nobody knows who you are. So it's easier to just piggyback off the people that do. In this case, these were podcasters, influencers, publications, et cetera. And working with them, building a relationship with them that is the basis of what can be for your startup as well. So the other thing I want to say is the focus here is on startup PR, and there are certain key advantages that you have as a startup that large companies don't.

And one of those key advantages is that you can take bigger risks. So to demonstrate this, I want to highlight what happened with Bud Light. Now, Bud Light raised a lot of controversy because they align themselves with this controversial influencer, a trans influencer whose face was put on the Bud Light cans. A lot of people started boycotting the product and a lot of publicity was generated from this, good or bad. And one of the reasons that Bud Light perhaps was able to take this big risk was because you had a brand that was in decline. And when something's in decline, you're more inclined to take risks to resurrect it. But usually when you're dealing with big brands or big companies, they don't want to take risks.

They have something to lose. They have brand equity. They have equity on their balance sheets. But when you're a startup, you don't have anything, so there's nothing to lose. That means that the advantage you have is you can take much bigger, bolder bets because nobody knows who you are. You have no reputation. You have no assets, you have nothing to lose, and you can't go negative unless you go into debt. So really, this is the strategy that you should be taking with your PR. Your PR is big, bold, risky bets because that's going to help you generate a lot of buzz, generate a lot of awareness, etcetera. Another key advantage is the David versus Goliath stories.

People love underdog stories. Underdog stories are more likely to be picked up by the media. So you can really piggyback off of that. And a large brand is not going to have an easy time being able to tell that story. And later in the Book, we'll get into details about storytelling elements and different ways to craft your message. Now the other thing is you can be more creative. You can also be much faster with putting things out. So you can come up with creative responses to trends that are happening. Whereas a giant company not can't necessarily do that because it's like moving the Titanic. It's a very slow, cumbersome process.

There's a lot of political approvals that need to go through Vpps ET cetera. So it's very hard to do things that are creative and bold. It's also very hard to do things that are fast, small, agile companies with a CEO or the head of PR or the head of marketing can just stamp something right away and approve it. You can get it out the door with something that's going to get a lot of attention. Now, the other key advantage you have over large companies is that you can focus on a hyper niche, a very narrow audience, a very narrow product category, and you can concentrate all your effort on that. Now, I was recently talking to Bruce Greenwald, who's one of the most renowned business professors at Columbia Business School.

He's known for analyzing value investors like Warren Buffett, a very intelligent man. And what he was saying was that with startups often really what you need to do is take a very narrow product range or very narrow product category. And that's really the only way that you can be operationally efficient, because often startups don't benefit from real economies of scale. They're not benefiting from customer captivity either. So competitive advantages strategically often don't exist with startups. But what does exist is operational efficiency, which often comes from having very hyper focused attention on certain types of things. Whereas with big companies, big companies need big markets, they need big growth, they need to start expanding in different directions.

And what that means is they lose their focus. So as a startup, you can kind of dominate the conversation, dominate the PR around a narrow scope, and that's going to be great for you. It's going to have a big impact for you, but it's not big enough for the big companies because it's just a drop a pebble in the ocean of their financials. So your big problem as a startup is really that nobody's ever heard of you. You have a huge awareness problem now. A lot of people in startup marketing don't really get this often. They're timid, they're conservative. They're worried about losing. They're worried about their reputation, They're worried about their brand.

That's the opposite approach that you need to have because your big problem is not what people think of you, like what your reputation is, what your positioning is. It's really that nobody's thinking about you at all. People are thinking about Nike all the time. They're thinking about Apple all the time. They're not thinking at all about your startup. So anything that you can do that generates huge awareness that puts you on the map is probably worth pursuing because it's going to overcome that huge hurdle of lack of awareness. So what does that mean? That means you can take risks because if you take risks, let's say you cold email a journalist at the New York Times and you're worried, Oh, what if he doesn't like it? Am I being too aggressive or am I blah, blah, blah? You got to wipe your mind out of that because tomorrow they're going to forget all about you.

Why? Because you have no awareness. So take those risks. Do anything you can to try to raise that awareness in ethical ways. Of course. The other thing I want to say is that there is a circus here. So what you want to do is you want to put on a show, you want to put on a spectacle, kind of like a scene here with Cirque du Soleil. It's not really about substance. So there are a lot of choices. And as a business person, as a trained manager, I'm looking at a lot of the stories that come out and I'm like, Well, that doesn't make sense. Why? Why are they focusing on that? That's a tiny market. Well, the reason they're doing those things is to put on a show to get media attention, because the media attention is very valuable.

So it seems some of the choices seem highly irrational. They don't align with the product positioning. But when you think about it in terms of media attention, it makes absolute sense. So I want to give you an example. Sometimes companies like Oreo or brands like

Oreo, they'll come up with these flavors, flavors that perhaps nobody would ever want, or maybe they'll only try it once. And it's like, Well, why would you invest heavily in a brand that is going to be not very popular at all? Well, the reason is to get publicity, right? The big, bold new flavor is going to get a lot of media attention. When Hines released Purple and Weird Colored Ketchups. I don't know how well it did.

Probably not very well because I don't see it on the store shelves anymore, but I'm sure it probably got a lot of immediate attention because it was exciting news. It was a spectacle. So really what happens when Oreo does something like this is it elevates the original Oreo sales, even though nobody may be buying the Cherry Cola Oreos, but it doesn't matter. Again, PR is the circus. It's about the show, not about the substance. So as a startup, one of the key things that you really want to do is you want to get creative and want to give you a few very specific examples of this. One is you can make your own ranking, so I'll give you an example of me doing this growth hacking approach when I was younger. I probably wouldn't do it today because it's a little bit suspicious.

But what I would do was I would run ads for a web design agency that I was running PPC, Google Bing ads, and instead of sending them to my landing page or my home page, what I did was I created a list of the top Web design firms, the top ten Web design firms. And I put my company, I think, at number one or number two. And then, Of course, people are already believing that this is one of the top Web design agencies. Now, I'm not recommending you do this, but this is when I was younger, I was a little more creative and experimental and just sort of hacking things out. And it was very effective. So you can create your own ranking. You can say, we're the best. The list of the best cat food brands, the list of the best waterproof pillows, whatever niche that you're in, create a list, own the list, publish a list.

Maybe it's an annual thing. So an example of this was US news. US News puts out rankings of colleges and universities, and that's why I ended up at the Kellogg School of Management. It was consistently ranked number one for marketing year after year. But recently there's been this controversy around how suspicious the ranking methodology is. Yale University and Yale Law School have withdrawn, even though Yale Law School was consistently ranked the top law school. But what this tells you is that lists feel secure. They feel like they're objective, but really they're not. They're just something that some organization came up with. And there's no reason that you can't come up with your own list as well.

That's a creative thing you can do. Another creative thing you can do is you can invent a special day. So national, whatever day. National Day, for example, was invented by this person, Colleen Page, who was an animal welfare advocate, and she invented National Pet Day in 2006. There's no reason you can't do that within your niche as well. Another thing that you can do is you can invent your own words. So HubSpot, for example, invented this word inbound marketing. And it's a word that has spawned many conversations in the marketing world today, inbound versus outbound. Personally, I'm a huge fan of outbound marketing. I think it's much more efficient and fast. But inbound marketing is certainly incredibly useful in a lot of contexts.

But basically HubSpot was able to invent a word, own that word and create a lot of publicity around it. Another example here I saw on the news Trump warns the biggest threat is nuclear warming. So there's a lot of people worried about global warming. So what he's done, or whoever wrote this article has done or wrote his speech has come up with this idea. Well, let's take this idea that's in people's minds of global warming and apply it to something else, which is the threat of nuclear war with Russia. And so he's coined this phrase nuclear warming, which is an interesting creative way of generating PR And

Of course, Donald Trump is a master of PR, and that's one of the reasons he was successful, despite not having as much funding as his competitors, he's able to get the the financial benefit of PR of free media attention, which is something you can do as a startup. You don't have a lot of money.

Well, you can leverage free PR to generate the equivalent of millions and millions of dollars in advertising. Now. There a general framework that we're going to use, a formula that we're going to use for this Book? And it's a formula I came up with. It's called the Three R's formula for startup PR, And those three S's are soliciting storytelling and scaling. Soliciting is basically reaching out to journalists, reaching out to influencers, reaching out to media outlets, and finding out who the people are that you need to contact. The second is storytelling. This is where you're crafting the message. You're coming up with some sort of compelling narrative that is going to resonate with people and that's going to be valuable for the journalists or the media. And then lastly, we're going to talk about scaling, which is going to comprise a variety of different things. But some of those things are going to be automation. So things like automated cold outreach and also some tricks like growth hacking and virality. So let's jump into the Book and let's continue.

Easy Public Relations Pitch- HARO

I'm going to give you an example of an extremely short but extremely effective pitch to the media. I get about three emails per day from Haro solicitations for people that want to get featured in the media. So in the business chapter, there was this one we were looking to interview successful Book creators. The requirements must be a Book creator. Run a digital training company, you must have a running website and have seen some success.

So within a day or two I got a response from the journalist and they said great! Send me a short email. They also sent me a word document with 27 different questions. So within a morning I just answered all of those questions. I sent the answers to all the questions in an email, and I also linked to a Google doc in case you prefer to Google Doc. So there you have it, a one sentence pitch to the media to get published for an interview through Haro.

Pay Journalists Directly

It can be very expensive to get into top publications. It might cost you $11,000, for example. One of the easiest workarounds through this is to communicate directly with a journalist. Now you can compile a database of journalists. You could reach out to people in your network. But one of the easiest things to do is just contact journalists through Haro, help a reporter out, explain your situation, and try to find out the price that that journalist is going to charge. So you can actually pay journalists directly to publish articles that you're interested in getting published. Now, the key thing here is that these journalists have spent a lot of time writing articles for publications, sometimes for no money at all.

So now that they have editorial rights to those websites, to those blogs, to those publications, one way that they're able to monetize that credential, that expertise is to charge to get articles published on the site. Now, this might seem a little bit deceptive or under the table. And what I will say, it's a nice workaround from the sticker price of paying $11,000 for an article to get published. But the other thing is that they're taking responsibility for it. So if the article is going to fall under that journalist's name, then they have to make sure that it's of high caliber.

So there is a vetting process there. And in that sense, it's a very authentic way of getting out there and getting on those top publications without doing something that is necessarily labeled as a sponsored post, which may get nixed by Google as they have been optimizing their algorithm accordingly. 17. $1M in 12 Days: Case Study "After only being in business 12 days, Ultra Right is expected to surpass $1 million in sales by Sunday, gaining over 10,000 customers and selling 20,000 six-packs since the April launch."

Source: Fox Business One of the biggest advantages startups have is their tolerance for high risk because they have nothing to lose. In addition, they're able to move quickly and capitalize on public relations trends such as the Bud Light transgender influencer controversy.

The highly controversial example above demonstrates how profitable it is for startups to take risks, capitalize on a trend, and take a bold stance even if it alienates a lot of people. 18. Concept Cars Concept cars seem like a waste of resources because they raise awareness for products that aren't even available for purchase. What they do, however, is garner a lot of incredibly valuable media attention for car brands. Startups can employ the same strategy with bold, innovative designs that may be unprofitable initially until one factors in the gains from publicity. With PR, performance matters more than substance.

In marketing strategy, one must consider not only the customer value proposition, but how value is created for collaborators such as journalists and influencers.

Consider the Bentley concept car below, which is fundamentally useless to customers but provides tons of media juice.

Source: CNBC

Soliciting for Public Relations 1

My formula for success with a startup is called the Three S's, and one of those S's is soliciting. Soliciting basically means reaching out to journalists, to reporters, to influencers, to publications to get them to run your story. And there are basically three key aspects to this. The first is research. This is where you're finding out which publications you're going to solicit, who are the influencers you're going to approach, and who are the journalists that you're interested in working with? The other key aspect of research is figuring out what types of content they like, what structure they like.

So, for example, do they prefer anecdotes, personal stories, or do they prefer things like original research or perhaps more technical information like testing one product against another? The other thing to look at is what is the submission process? Larger publications are probably going to have a more formalized process to approach them with your story. Now the second aspect of soliciting is what I call list building. This is where you're compiling or buying lists of people and publications that influence your target. So, for example, you might be particularly interested in getting in big publications, things like CNN and TechCrunch, but often the most profitable publications to be in might be ones you've never heard of but are particularly popular among your target audience.

And those smaller niche publications might actually be more hungry for content because it may be harder to get more detailed content stories or analyses, things like that. So make sure you do your research to make sure that you're not just intuitively guessing what the best publications and journalists are going to be, but you're actually finding out quantitatively. And one of the tools I'm going to talk about later, Of course, is Sparktoro. Now, the third aspect of soliciting is actually contacting and reaching out to these people and publications. You can do this through email. You can do it through direct mail. If you want to be really aggressive, you can also do it through DMS. So I've had success sending direct messages through things like Facebook and Instagram.

You can phone publications and journalists, you can meet people in person at things like trade shows. You can ask for referrals, maybe you have a mutual contact on LinkedIn or a mutual contact through a lawyer or some other professional or consultant. I've had a lot of success also going to the admins of groups. So for example, Facebook group admins are going to be thought leaders and people that are going to be great for publishing content, people who are running Reddit groups, people that are having conversations on Quora. And if all else fails, really what you can do is you can just go to the contact page on the publication website, the journalists or the influencer website and submit the form right then and there.

Now, one of the things I want to say about a lot of PR in the startup space is that it's basically outbound sales or outbound business development. And if you're not familiar with these terms, basically outbound sales is sending cold emails, doing cold calls, that type of thing, where you're reaching out to people. And usually what you're doing in cases like that with outbound sales is you're trying to get people to buy your product. But in this case, what you're doing is you're really selling a story. You're not selling a product, you're selling a story, and they don't even need to pay for it. So you're selling a free story, but you're asking them to give up their resources in terms of publication and editing, etcetera, to run with your story.

And that's going to take a lot of persuasion, a lot of convincing. Now in the startup world in general, with marketing, it's very easy to get excited about big, bold things rebranding, making a grand website, running fancy advertising, etcetera. But often when you really want to get some hard performance, you really want to get sales. One of the best approaches is outbound sales, just sending cold emails. It's not flashy, it's just text. It's just a conversation. That's really the closest you can come to getting a sale. Now, similarly with PR, it's easy to get excited about getting a PR agency or we're going to get this. We're going to do a huge PR stunt in Madison Square Avenue, or we're going to get the Times Square Giant Digital Board, or we're going to do something grand and big.

But really, what's going to get success initially is going to be that boring sexy thing of just writing a text email to a journalist, to a publication, and that's probably where you're going to be spending a lot of your time with startup PR. 20. TEMPLATE to pitch bloggers/journalists. Examples of good and bad pitches to bloggers/journalists from the book "Stop Chasing Influencers"

BAD PITCH Hello so and so, I'm a huge fan of your blog. The content is great.I would love to give back by writing a guest post for your audience. Do you take guest posts? GOOD PITCH Hello so and so, I'm a fan of your website. My favorite article is "Name a specific article that has helped you." I have written a guest post that speaks to your audience, which is at the bottom of this email. (Bloggers hate attachments. Send the post in the body of the e-mail.) Here are some samples of my work on these websites (name a few places you've guest posted and hyperlink the articles). Thank you,

Your name is 21. Getting Published in Major Publications How to get easily published in major publications 1. Pay for direct-sponsored posts/articles. These can cost a minimum of say a few hundred dollars up to $3,000, as provided in a media kit that you request. The challenge with this approach is the lengthy approval process and queue. For reference, I am currently working on an article that costs $900-$1,000 to get published while my assistant works on the draft. 2. Pay people with editorial access. Some people spend years writing for publications for free and eventually earn the right to editorial access to major publications. These people then monetize their editorial access by charging people you and me to have their articles published. This approach is faster than paying for a direct sponsored post. You typically pay less in Asia and more in other regions such as Europe.

A typical fee is $800-$1100 in my experience.

This is NOT a bribe and does NOT violate policies with the publication. 3. Evaluating publications. Below is an example of how I compared various publications for an article opportunity. Using Similarweb data estimates:

MSN - 690.5* M - 4.5% into software/tech

Chicago Tribune - 11.5 m - 5.8% into software/tech

WashingtonTimes- 3.4 m - 5.97% into software/tech

Digital Journal- 900k - 50% into software/tech

Hackernoon - 2.4m - 9.66% into software/tech

4. Cheaper opportunities.

Starting at 200 USD per release, you can get exposure on USA news sites like Fox, CNET and OTA platforms like ABC etc. These publications last 90 days.

*= Monthly visits in millions All website visitors above are male dominant, and a larger percentage are within the range of 25-34, worldwide audience with larger percentage from USA—————————————————————————————————

of the big advantages of getting articles published like this is the quality of the backlink to help with your SEO and domain authority. These backlinks are less useful, however, if the page you are optimizing already has substantial backlinks from high-authority publications (e.g., your Amazon product listing). 22. Startup PR Case Study: Luggage The "meta strategy" of marketing often involves designing products more for PR than for actual customers.

In other words, you don't necessarily create product features because customers are demanding them, but because you know you'll get a lot of attention or word-of-mouth by doing so. When you position your product around a good story, it makes it a lot easier to reach out to the media to get a story about you. Take for example "Crash Baggage," luggage that comes pre-dented. I'm sure there's an element of customer value here, but I think the real benefit is the innate storytelling built into this product. Lots of people will spread the word about luggage that comes pre-dented, and the media is far more likely to run a story on this than on some generic luggage brand. You might think "what a pointless product feature." But from the perspective of PR, it makes a lot of sense.

Easiest Way to Get Published - HARO (Help A Reporter Out)

One of the single easiest ways to get published in major publications is to use a reporter.com. So this is to help a reporter out, also known as Haro. And when you go to this website what you're going to do is register. I'm a source and it's very easy. What's going to happen is you're going to start getting emails, and these emails are going to contain articles that are coming out where the journalist or the reporter needs a reference. They need somebody who is an expert in a given topic to make a contribution to the article that they're writing. So, for example, I recently received this one here, and you can see that the different articles are categorized. So in biotech and health care we're looking for anti-inflammatory slow cooker recipes you can make on Sunday. ET cetera. ET cetera.

So this person is looking for a doctor on the risk of cancer from supplements. Now, if we go down to business wire interpersonal skills. Important in 2024. So if you're an expert in interpersonal communications or you want to establish yourself as an influencer, what you could do is select this and send an email out to this person explaining what these interpersonal skills are and why they're important in 2024. So it's one thing to randomly solicit journalists, but when you solicit them based on precisely what they're looking for. In other words, these journalists are in the market for specific types of expertise. Then they're going to be much more receptive to what you have to say. And you could get published in many different publications using this method.

15 HARO Rules

RL is one of the easiest ways to get published in major publications. However, you need to follow the rules. Rule number one sources will receive three emails a day. That's right, three emails per day. These are going to be requests from reporters and media outlets. You're going to scan them if you're knowledgeable about any of the topics. What you're going to do is you're going to email the anonymous email that's provided for that particular inquiry and explain why you're a good fit for it, or follow whatever the rules are for that particular listing. Number two sources must have clear, reasonable expertise in a topic relevant to the query. So since I'm a marketing expert, I tend to respond mostly to those regarding marketing, branding, digital marketing. ET cetera. Now, if you are representing a client, then make sure that your client has relevant expertise and do not waste the journalist's time explaining that you're representing the client.

Number three sources must send their own unique responses when replying to journalists' source requests. Sending a journalist plagiarized content will result in termination. Also, keep in mind that a lot of the journalists now are going to be very clear that they don't want anything AI generated to not spam reporters with off-topic pitches and responses to their queries. Five sources may not require backlinks link swaps in exchange for their use of their pitch. Now keep in mind you are going to be wanting to get backlinks. Just don't push too aggressively for this. Do not pitch products unless you're specifically asked to do so.

Seven you may forward queries to others via email or social media, so if you find somebody else that's an expert in a particular area, you can lend them a hand by saying, this is a good place for you to get some credibility, some publicity, some backlinks. Eight you're not allowed to harvest any reporter information provided in the emails for any reason. Nine reply to source requests with complete relevant answers to the question, including a short bio and your contact info. Do not reply to source requests with incomplete information or solely or solely. Would you like to talk about this? Then if you were replying to a source request on behalf of your client, directly reply with your client's response. Do not reply solely with my client. Can speak about this.

Don't waste their time. 11 do not include attachments, attachments or automatically deleted through the system. If you have relevant supplemental information or collateral that is helpful to the story, use a service like Dropbox to send links to the reporters in your pitch. 13 anonymous queries are often larger outlets that choose to anonymize their listings to alleviate spam. Reply to those queries. As detailed above, 14 media professionals are encouraged to perform additional due diligence prior to pitching. 15 be excellent to each other. There is a very short pitch I did.

Somebody said they were looking under the business chapter for an expert in branding, so I responded with a very quick email. Branding expert x PlayStation Brand Manager. Hi there, I was a global brand manager for Sony PlayStation and studied brand management at the Kellogg School of Management. I'd be happy to help with some data driven branding insights. Now, depending on the situation, you probably want to add more information in a lot of those spiels that you're going to be delivering. But don't send any attachments. And what Horo is going to do is they're going to give you an email address that's specific to Horo, that is going to go directly to the relevant journalist or reporter for that particular reference.

Sample HARO Pitch

I'm going to give you another example of a pitch that I sent out. Here was the email that came in. I found one that seemed particularly interesting to me, which was innovative marketing in the gaming world from Anonymous Media Outlet. We're exploring groundbreaking marketing strategies in the gaming industry, and they're trying to get a glimpse of gaming marketing trends for the next level of player engagement. So I'm a very credible source for this because I was a global brand manager for Sony PlayStation, was the director of marketing for Ironclad Games. Here's the pitch that I decided to send out.

Now, what I want to note here is that I added more detail than I would with something like getting an interview, because often what Harrow publishers really want is just something they can copy and paste as a quote and insert it quickly into whatever article that they're pasting, and then they might throw in a reference to you and hopefully a backlink. So this is a case where I provide my thought leadership very quickly in the morning before I go out for a run. So I said hi. I was a global brand manager for Sony PlayStation and our director of marketing for Ironclad Games, a link to my website. So I'm just quickly establishing my credibility. And then I talk about influencers. I had PewDiePie review one of my games, and receive 14 million views.

I also talked about another campaign that I ran with Micro-influencers, and then I see, say, the biggest mistake that I see in marketing is the agile mindset, where game marketers are being influenced too much by what's happening in the software industry. Then I talk about how entertainment marketing is different. I cite some research here from Harvard Business School. I also cite some research from Byron Sharp, and add my own thoughts to both of these, and how some research is applicable in some contexts and not others. And then I conclude by saying that the two big things people can do is piggyback off the credibility of influencers and invest heavily in launch week. So don't spread out your marketing budget, concentrate it in the short period around product launch.

So I'm adding a lot of information, but I wrote it very quickly as something that can quickly get published into this report. 26. HARO PR Pitch Templates from DigiGrow Reference: Digigrow.co (A) HARO PITCH THAT GOT A DR(DOMAIN RATING) 81 BACKLINK

Hi Spela, 1) The most important report I use for clients is the Goal Completions Report. Why do I use this report? This report gives my clients an idea of how many leads I generated for them. This report has a direct correlation with the Return on Investment I delivered for my clients. How to set-up this report? Once you log into Google Analytics, follow this path: Admin > View > Goals Next click on New Goal as shown in this image[1]. You can then proceed to set your goal as per your client's requirements.

How to track this report? Wait for at least a month before you check the report. This gives the tool enough time to collate metrics and provide you with a complete picture. Then head over to the Conversions tab on Google Analytics, click on Goals and then click on Overview. This image[2] gives a better idea. 2) Yes, I use Google

---

1. https://lh5.googleusercontent.com/

   3DqRfHNIaEp2jzCsVq3e8tC3yERivdV0YZCJjq5WfPuE--

   QWzaFIVudBp5trZ35Ub0wn7ShOmgdmw6WMULYKjvMMEKlkgsX_TgLyp07LEgfyxK

   xzIyH_0DKpxUi86Dl8woTU957v

2. https://lh3.googleusercontent.com/

   UQBMuo6qs4GKPEhyfwWM79sdwCEQyBlCyPuk2GZcdbK0ZoovNAf0VWix0XNUFv

Analytics reports for my clients ————————- Please let me know if you have any questions. I'm happy to answer them all. — Thank you Anurag Surya Owner | Digital Marketing Manager DigiGrow[3] (B) HARO PITCH THAT GOT A DR62 BACKLINK

Hi Tracey, Please find my response to your HARO query below. — Most small businesses rely on Google Ads to generate leads. However, the conversion from Ads reduces during inflation because their potential leads have a lower inclination to spend.

This means their cost per click goes off the roof. The best way to reduce paid Ad expenses is by investing in SEO. A good SEO strategy will help you rank on the first page of Google search pages without investing in CPC Ads. — Thank you Anurag Surya Owner | Digital Marketing Manager DigiGrow[4] (C) HARO PITCH TEMPLATE FOR INTERVIEW REQUESTS

Hi [Journalist"s Name], I am [Your Name], the [Your Title] at [Your Company], and have [Years of Experience] in [Niche]. I have written/spoken on [The Topic] for [Publication/Conference] and would be happy to share my thoughts with you or your audience. I am available at [Preferred time slot] and can provide additional materials – links to relevant articles or a short bio.

Let me know if you want to connect. Happy to work on another time slot. Let me know, Thank you for considering my pitch. Best regards, [Your Name] [Position] [Company Name] [LinkedIn Profile URL] (D) HARO PITCH TEMPLATE FOR QUOTE REQUESTS

RhqttztWM_EJweyHnl9A_LO5m60yZCkz2Xwzl1xgOOrwhH4_2jbIAUH08eYoe3cDYG v56R4y_C

3. https://digigrow.co/

4. https://digigrow.co/

Hi [Journalist's name], My name is [Your Name] and I am the [Your Role] at [Your Company]. I have an experience of [X] years with [Niche]. Please see my response to your HARO query below ================ [HARO Pitch] ================ Please let me know if you have any follow-up questions. — Thank you [Your Name] [Designation] [Headshot] [Company Name] (E) TYPICAL HARO PITCH

Hello [redacted],

Here's another pitch from a HARO source! Hope you find the perfect match for your story.

Best,

The HARO Team

Source Contact Info:

- Name: [redacted]
- Email: [redacted]
- Company: [redacted]
- Phone: [redacted]

Pitch Title: HARO - Employee Empowerment Tips w Implement

Pitch Content:

Hello [redacted],

1. How do you empower your employees to make crucial career decisions?

The best way to encourage employees to make crucial career decisions is by **providing honest and fact-based feedback**. It gives them the information they need to choose their career paths wisely. Knowing where they excel and fail is an opportunity to persevere or improve.

2. What is the best way to convey the roles and responsibilities to a new employee? We're particularly keen to hear from companies that would be open to follow-up questions

- Start as early as the **recruitment process** to create a cohesive employee experience. If they know what to expect during the early stages of the process, they are most likely to set their career goals and determine whether it aligns with the company's values and branding.
- The **onboarding process** is the next thing to consider because it coaches them to make decisions based on the company's culture and work ethic.

Is this all you require?

Regards,

[redacted]
Founder & [redacted]
Website URL: https://[redacted]
Headshot URL: https://[redacted]
LinkedIn: https://www.linkedin.com/in/[redacted]

Track and Respond: https://[redacted]

Want to let the source know their pitch will not be used? Click here to say "No thanks!"

If this pitch is not relevant, click here

1. Source's contact information 2. Pitch title 3. Pitch content 4. Source's signature 5. A unique URL that the journalist can use to respond to the source 6. An option for the journalist to escalate impertinent queries to HARO

Soliciting for Public Relations 2

I mentioned that a lot of startup PR is really just hitting those emails, reaching out, trying to convince people to run with your story. But sometimes the solicitations involve more of a formal submission process. So an example of this would be an award submission to become the best web designer or one of the top medical practitioners in your given city. These types of things. An example that I have displayed here is HubSpot. So if you're in the marketing and sales space, one of the most popular places to be published is going to be the HubSpot blog. And you can see here they have a very detailed application process to follow where everything is laid out clearly about what they're looking for and how to submit your written content. They're going to say things like, We really like original research, so you can really cater to their needs in that way.

So as with outbound sales, outbound PR in the startup world is going to come with a small conversion rate. So you're going to really need to solicit way more journalists and publications than you expect to be published in. Now, a certain fraction of those people are going to respond and a fraction of the people that respond are actually going to end up ultimately publishing your content or featuring your chapter, whatever it is that you've created. From my experience, you generally want to follow up at least once. Now, a lot of people are going to say, oh, you need to follow up seven times, ten times, and we're going to talk later about how to automate those types of things.

But what I would say anecdotally is that try to get at least one follow up and make sure that that follow up isn't just, hey, bumping this to the top of your inbox. It's not just, hey, just following up, but in your follow up message, make sure you're actually saying something of value, perhaps just summarizing what you said in the initial email, the initial cold email. So for example, this is what I did when I was approaching the top influencers in the veterinary space. I sent a message to the top influencer in North America for veterinarians, and I simply sent one follow up email and that's where the partnership got started. So that one follow up is often all you really need, or even the initial email is enough.

Now I'm going to highlight a few notes from the book. Free PR If you haven't read or listened to the audiobook version, it's something you may want to check out and here are some of those key things to keep in mind. So for every 100 pitches, you might get five story placements. So again, just setting the expectation that you need to reach more people than you actually need. Journalists receive about 100 emails per day, so you need to make sure that you have something compelling and ideally catered to the specific type of content that they want to be able to get their attention. An example of a solicitation verbatim would be something like I enjoyed your article about X, so whatever that topic was, I thought you'd be interested in a new solution.

And then you can go into detail about why your product, why your service is a good fit for and aligns well with other articles that this person has published. Now a verbatim for what your follow up message might be would be something like What do you think of the story idea? I'd greatly appreciate feedback or suggestions. So one of the great things about this type of script is that you're encouraging them to reply and you're not. You're not asking for a hard promise of Will you run with this story? You don't seem that needy. You're just sort of softly asking for feedback or suggestions. And that response is the key to getting the conversation started and hopefully getting a long term relationship started ultimately. And one of the things pointed out in this book also is that relationships get easier over time.

So once you get that initial story, once you get that conversation started, it's going to get easier and easier and easier to get published. Once you're published in one magazine, it's going to be easier to get the second one and so on. The other key thing is having small tasks. So for example, instead of just saying, Hey, will you run the story, it's more like, Hey, would you mind introducing me to the producer instead of being like, Hey, can I, can you promise to get me on the show? So small asks Small promises can really help get the process lubricated. So part of the solicitation process is really just getting the research, trying to figure out who to contact, what they like to publish, and then catering your pitch around that.

So one of the keys is to look at where your competitors and your partners are getting published and reach out to the authors that have published content about them. So, for example, I did a search here for A2 accounting and you can see I went to the new chapter. I'm able to see where they're getting published. They're getting published in the CPA Canada, which is perhaps the most prestigious accounting organization in Canada. And you can see, okay, well, they publish content, so maybe we can get published there as well. And we can use the credibility of the CPA brand in future marketing and see this site I've never heard of called Beta Kit, also published content on this New Zealand company Software Advice.

You can just go through the news here and see if you're interested in getting published in any of those places your competitors were also published in. So with the research, it's up to you how detailed and how formalized you want to get with this. So one thing you could do is interview your current customers or just the target audience that you want and try to find out where they go to get information. What kind of media do they follow? You could also survey them so you could use a tool like I showcased here called Sentiment. And in my experience, it's about $15 per response and you'll probably get

100 responses to get people and find out who your target audience follows in terms of media, in terms of influencers.

Or you could create your own survey using Google forms for free. Sentiment, for example, provides their own data collection forms, but you could use any sort of survey tool. SurveyMonkey is another example. Now I'm going to walk through a tutorial later, but Sparktoro is going to be an excellent place to first put in information about who your target audience is and it'll spit out the publications, influencers, podcasts, etcetera, which is where you're also want to you're going to want to get published. And you can also use this to do some competitor, Intel. Now one of the keys with solicitations and this is based on quantitative data research from Dongbu Yeo is you don't want to be too aggressive.

You don't want to be like just like when you're selling a product, you don't want to be like, Hey, do you want to buy my product? Or, Hey, do you have 15 minutes for a meeting? What you want to do is have a softer ask, which is basically asking for interest. Does this store interest you or is this the kind of thing that your audience might be interested in instead of, Hey, will you run my store? Or Hey, will you meet with me? Way too aggressive. It's a huge turnoff. In my experience, most outreach, most cold outreach is way too aggressive, way too annoying. And as an influencer myself, I'm bombarded with messages from people that are just always trying to get something out of me. Hey. Hey. Would you like to have a meeting right away? Hey, hey, hey.

Are you interested in buying? And it's just. It comes across very unempathetic. But when you ask people for interest, you have more empathy. And sometimes what you may even want to do is pay them for their time. So if the journalist is very popular, you can say, Hey, I'll give you $100. I just want to get your thoughts on this story idea that I had. I'm new to PR and I don't know if this is something that journalists are interested in. So what you're doing when you pay people for their time is you're saying, I respect your time. I understand you're getting 100 emails per day.

And because of that, I'm going to reimburse you for your advice. So you can see here the research where when you have a specific CTA, which is like, do you have 15 minutes on Tuesday? Not a very effective approach, open ended CTAs, which is, hey, do you have time to meet next week? Something like that. Not very effective. What's most effective is just trying to see if people have some sort of interest in what you're pitching them and you're going to get a higher response rate. You're going to get a high meeting rate, you're going to get a much higher placement rate.

And again, the research is coming from Gongyo. Now I have a detailed tutorial later in the Book where I walk through step by step how to do this. But one of the best ways to get contact information for my experience is using LinkedIn. Now you could just use LinkedIn people. If you go to their contact information, you're able to see their emails. A lot of the time not everybody puts their contact information, but a lot of people do. And a more formal way of doing this is using LinkedIn Sales Navigator, which is a paid premium feature within LinkedIn. So what you can do is you can find people using keywords like journalist, blogger, influencer, reporter, or you can do a search for an industry such as media and entertainment.

And then what it'll do, Sales Navigator is it'll spit out a list of people who meet these criteria. So what you could do is you could build a list of journalists, publications, et cetera influencers, and use that as your solicitation group. And another level of complexity that you don't have to do but is going to help you scale later is to use scrap IO. Let's scrap.io will scrape the emails from the people that you've collected and in Sales Navigator and it'll make it very easy to export that as a CSV. So as an Excel file, which then you can import into a cold email tool such as Lemlist. But again, I'll walk you through the technical details later. This is just a high level overview of how you can gather contact information of journalists using Sales Navigator.

One way to make it faster might be using scrap IO. Now, another thing to keep in mind is that you can reach out through social media and through people's contact pages. So just go to Twitter. A lot of journalists, reporters are very active on Twitter or go to their Instagram. There's no reason you cannot message them there. A lot of people think, oh, well, this is a formal outreach. I should only use email. No, these are media companies. These are influencers. They're active on social media. There's no reason you can't contact them through these channels, especially if the email is not that effective. Response rates are not that hot, that high. Now, if your response rate is really low, there's what I call the sledgehammer approach. You can see this picture of a sledge hammer where you're given everything to grab attention.

You're giving it all, and that is a direct mail box. So you can see this direct mail package I've borrowed from just to give credit here, but sending a giant 3D box with some free chocolates or a free mug, maybe a combination of little gifts, maybe a corporate umbrella from Duvec, something like that is going to get attention for sure. And it's going to get past the gatekeepers, if there are any. And what you can do is you can have a one sheet letter that sort of describes the story that you want to get published. You could even present them with a $50 Amazon gift card and say, hey, if you just can't get on the phone with me, give me some advice or, you know, tell me your interest in the story. I'll give you 50 bucks for your time.

This is the sledgehammer approach. If all else fails, you can send direct mail and you're highly likely to get a response rate because who's not going to remember a giant gift box that they got almost like a Christmas gift that came in the mail. And one of the things to keep in mind with this direct mail is don't just send it alone. What you want to do is you want to sandwich it between emails. So send emails to follow up and say, Hey, I hope you enjoyed the package I sent you. Once again, my story is about X, Y, Z, and I'm wondering if you have some time to chat about it. Here's a link to schedule time or just ask them to reply if they're interested. So you can get a meeting set up to discuss it further or even just chat about it through email.

Great aggressive approach, especially if you're going after high caliber influencers. You know, like Oprah Winfrey or Suze Orman or some other high profile people in your niche, they're probably not going to be that big, but maybe they're pretty busy people. Now, one of the things you're going to be asking for is not going to be as clear as this is a specific story. What you might be asking for is a speaking engagement. So here's an example of one that I was able to get when I was working for this company. Web agility was when I had the CEO as a guest speaker for a webinar with an advisor and tips from an Amazon insider on how to scale it to a $20 million business.

So one of the key things here is when you're looking for speaking engagements, it may be at big events or trade shows, etcetera, but sometimes really what you're doing is you're just looking for people or publications that have bigger reach than you do. So it's fine to publish your own webinars, it's fine to publish your own email publications. ET cetera. But really, if you want to get a wide reach, you have to find the people with bigger reach. And in this instance, advisors had a wider reach with Amazon sellers. So this was a way I was able to reach them, was by soliciting them for a speaking engagement, a virtual speaking engagement in this case. Now another example where I did this successfully was soliciting veterinarian podcasts.

Now I worked for this Google accelerator startup where we did have we were affiliated with the podcast, but I was able to leverage that credibility to solicit all the biggest podcasts veterinarians followed and we were able to get tons of free speaking engagements to get on the air, talk about our product, talk about the product story, the company story, and basically what these were were speaking engagements again for the CEO of the company, which is what you can do with webinars as well. Now another example of where we can see the effectiveness of speaking engagements is with personal branding. So here is a case study and you can want to give credit here to the website where I've gotten this case study on Jordan Peterson.

Now, Jordan Peterson is a Canadian professor who was just kind of a, you know, a credible professor. And he became super famous. And one of the reasons he became so famous was because of getting essentially what our guest speaking opportunities were. So you can see the spikes in his popularity and his subscriptions when he was featured on Joe Rogan twice. Joe Rogan being perhaps the most popular podcaster. You can also see what happened when he got on the Rubin report. He got on these other podcasts and then it really skyrocketed when he got on the Channel four News with Kathy Newman.

So really what you're doing with speaking engagements is you're piggybacking off existing audiences and just having that opportunity to talk on the air to their audience and really skyrocket your brand. And that's how Jordan Peterson was able to build a personal brand empire that made him very profitable, started getting him these giant book publishing deals, really leveraging these audiences, these influencers. And you can solicit them yourself. If you have a good story, you have something worth talking about. Maybe it's research that you did or an interesting story. Then you can get on the air.

I've done it too. I've been on guest podcasts, guest on YouTube channels. Sometimes they approach me, but you can build a whole system of approaching them and get a constant flow of free PR, free being. You're not paying for it, but you are paying for it in terms of your time and the research that needs to go into preparing the presentation.

SparkToro

So sparktoro it's free to a certain extent. I think you get something like ten searches per month and those searches, you can keep redoing the same searches. So the capacity is very generous. And what it does is it enables you to figure out who the key influencers are that carry a lot of clout with your target customers. It enables you to identify which media sources your target customers are using and to just generally put together what I would call an influencer marketing plan. It also kind of bridges into the space of PR. So let's take a look at how this would work. So the first thing is you want to create an account.

So do that. I've already done it. And then you have to define your audience. So there are different ways to do this. You can define it in terms of what words they use in their profile, what social accounts they follow, websites that they visit and frequently use hashtags that they have. Typically I use these words in their profile. So for example, let's say that the target audience was medical doctors. Well, I might put an MD here or I might put a physician surgeon, something like that. So let's just try a physician and see what happens. Okay. So it's doing the search, calculating the audience size, and we're getting some interesting data. So we start to see, okay, here are some of the social accounts that physicians follow.

Here's the websites, hidden gems, which are perhaps a good starting point. Now, when you reach out to influencers, it's going to be hard to get those Tier one people that are constantly being solicited. But the hidden gems might be an easier beachhead for you if you're just starting with influencer marketing and PR. Same thing hidden gems for websites. So websites may be easier to get like a guest blog post. It's probably going to be harder with these hardcore ones podcasts, so you can be a guest speaker on a podcast. You could have your guest speak on a podcast that's going to be much easier than building up your own podcast from scratch.

That's something that a lot of people say you should start your own podcast, start your own publication. But not all of us are journalists, and not all of us have the time to build up a massive following. It's much easier to just borrow a following that already exists. Similar Book of action with YouTube channels. And then there are press accounts where you might want to work with a PR agent or something. So we're looking at physicians as the target audience. We can get some insights about the audience, the size, certain hashtags that they're using. So all of this is very interesting, but where it really starts to get exciting is here look at the social accounts.

So these are the social accounts that they're following. So this guy is a surgeon who's an influencer. Let's take a closer look at him. All right. So Sparktoro gives them a score. You can see that most of his following is coming from Twitter. So one way you could use this is you could reach out to this person and say, Hey, we'd like to pay you to do a demo of our product. So you give this man $100, $75 to sit through a demo of your product to get his feedback. And once you kind of have some rapport with this person, then you can start to talk to him about, hey, you know, maybe we're interested in paying you to talk about our product through a tweet, right? He has a lot of clout on Twitter. He also has some clout on Facebook. So maybe you want to do a Facebook live with this person where he's showing your product.

Now, the way you reach out to influencers, it's not always explicitly sales oriented. It's not necessarily just talking about your product and paying them to promote your product. It might also be something that's a softer approach to marketing. It's, hey, are you interested in doing a joint webinar where we talk about solving a problem that the audience has and perhaps your product sponsors that content? So there's kind of a spectrum of ways to work with these people, ranging from high level content marketing, which is probably more appropriate for larger companies or companies that have a lot more funding to more bottom of the funnel things like product oriented webinars, sponsored demos, things like that. Okay.

So let's take a look at some of these other influencers. Now you can see that some of them are brand names. Not all influencers are individuals. So influencers are often associations, sometimes they're individuals, sometimes it's a brand or a brand that's associated with an individual. It really depends. But let's take a look at this other individual and we can see, okay, he has a pretty strong following on Twitter and Facebook, pretty minor following on Instagram, but this gives you some good ideas of how to reach the medical market through influencers. So this is the social category. But Of course, websites, which is a more conventional approach to get things like guests, blog posts.

You can look at some of these now. It's probably going to be pretty hard to get on there, so you might want to kind of start towards the bottom here and here you need to upgrade your account to see it, but that's fine. I mean, try it out, try out the free account, see if you get any traction and if it's worthwhile and you want to invest heavily in this space, then you can upgrade. Podcasts, I think, are a great way to get started here. You can reach out to any one of these podcasts and say, Hey, we want to be a guest on your show, and we have an expert who's probably the CEO of your company who's an authority on some topic and just offers to show up on their podcast.

Now, sometimes it may be pay to play, so you need to pay to have your podcast or to have your podcast published with them. Or it may just be a sponsorship, which I'm not a huge fan of sponsorships when it's just kind of the bulk of the content that has nothing to do with your product or nothing to do with the problem that your product solves. Instead, it's just, Hey, this is brought to you by brand name. Don't recommend that because the audience will just filter it out as an ad, It may work for some people. It hasn't worked for me. YouTube You can see the most popular channels now. Obviously, Mayo Clinic is probably not going to endorse your product, particularly if you're a startup, but if you're more established and you have a credible brand, it may be worth reaching out.

Now the press, we can see, okay, so these physicians, they follow the World Health Organization, New York Times, CNN, Harvard Health, so a lot of big brand names. It's going to be a little harder to break in there. So when you're going after more niche markets like smaller groups of people, what you're going to find is it gets easier. You're going to be looking at more niche publications, podcasts that don't have huge followings. It's probably going to be easier to get guest positions on these. So Sparktoro is an excellent tool as an entry point into marketing that I would say has large economies of scale. So there is this bias in marketing that has been promoted by companies such as HubSpot. And again, I have nothing against HubSpot. I think it's a great tool. I use it. I think they have tremendous support.

But this idea that inbound marketing and content marketing is everything, it leaves people in the wrong direction because it makes marketers and SaaS marketers in particular think they need to be publishers. They need massive amounts of blog posts, they need these engaging eBooks, they need long research reports. The problem with that approach is you probably do not have a large audience. You are not journalists, you are not newspaper writers. But there are people out there, these influencers, these podcasters, these bloggers who already have the audience. So it's much better to think about distribution. Okay, Creating content is one thing, but actually getting in front of people is another. And the easiest way to do that is through key influencers. And the easiest way to find key influencers is using Sparktoro.

Now what you might find is that a lot of the influencers that you're looking for aren't on here. And one thing that we know when we look at research from the University of Pennsylvania with Jonah Berger, who's one of the biggest names in the marketing space, because he wrote the book Contagious, he has another book about how to change people's minds called A Catalyst. And what we know from him and from other research is that most word of mouth is offline. And that makes it a challenge when you're finding key influencers because it's very difficult to track offline word of mouth conversations. So then you're going to be looking at things like other tools. So meetup.com, where people organize physical events, you're going to be looking at association presidents that host events and weekly meetings. A lot of the word of mouth engagements are going to happen there.

PR Storytelling 1

Another key element of the three formulas for startup is storytelling. Essentially, this is content creation. It could be in text, it could be in chapter, it could be on a podcast. It could pretty much be in any media that you choose. And for my experience, there are basically two types of content that are foolproof and are going to be great for getting attention. The first is a funding round, so if you're the kind of startup that's getting venture capital, then you get your series C or series D or series B that is 100% worthy of attention. Now, if something else happens in your company, like getting a new hire, I remember speaking to a PR expert in Silicon Valley about this and he was saying people are hiring people from credible companies all the time in Silicon Valley.

So former employees from Google, from Twitter, etcetera. And they said it's not really that newsworthy. Now in your niche, maybe it is more newsworthy. But if you're in Silicon Valley where there's a lot of huge tech companies and people are changing companies all the time, then not really that worthy of attention. Now, the second type of foolproof content, I would say, is original research. So if you've done some sort of study that the industry is going to value, even if it's just surveying, say, 100 people in the industry, that kind of thing is very easy to get published, whether it's just in a guest webinar, maybe you're just a guest speaker on a podcast talking about your research. But this type of thing, this type of original research is very easy to get media attention.

Now to more generalize the types of content or stories that you can come up with. We're going to rely on the book free PR, and the author has four categories of business stories. So the first is announcements. And later we're going to talk about why announcements are one of the key aspects of copywriting that are the most likely to get attention from readers. So these are things like launching a new product or service, forming a new partnership, a new hire, maybe somebody that's famous or most importantly, a new round of fundraising, as I mentioned earlier. So announcements are very time constrained, right? It's based around some sort of event that's happening, such as a product launch.

But then we have evergreen stories. These are things like how you did it, how you built that product, how you built that empire, how you built that charitable arm of your company. It's going to be the story behind the story. It's going to be things like weird rituals or fun aspects of your business or interesting aspects of your company culture, which might be particularly effective if you're trying to recruit employees. Next, We have seasonal things, so things that perhaps are associated with holidays. Maybe you did something like building robotic reindeer or maybe you're an egg company or a company that makes mayonnaise. Well, something around Easter makes the most sense because it's very seasonal.

If you're in retail and you get a quarter of your sales around Black Friday or Cyber Monday, then particular stories are going to be more relevant to the media around that time. And lastly, we have one content type for business stories that's completely under your control and that's stunts and events. And what you're doing here is you're capitalizing on some sort of an event such as South by Southwest or maybe it's a chapter game event or an industry event, and you're able to create some sort of stunt or attention grabbing thing for the event. So, for example, SPCA, puppies being brought to your show booth is going to be something that's going to garner a lot of media attention. So those are the four categories of business stories.

Now related to that is going to be five story angles, which also come from the book Free PR. So once you've decided what kind of story is most relevant to your business, to your product, to your service. Now it's how do you craft the narrative? Is the narrative overcoming adversity? This is going to be inspiring, inspiring aspects or a back story to your business? Is it going to be about culture? So things that set your company apart from competitors, that's the type of thing that a publication like Fast Company is going to be interested in publishing.

Is it going to be a company endorsement? So things like overcoming problems or achieving success, is it going to be about leveraging technology, which is going to be the kind of story angle that's appropriate for Trend Huntercombe or for TechCrunch? Or is the story angle going to be about the future? Maybe things like thought leadership, an inspirational future of where your company is headed, an origin story, the kind of thing that would get published on Wired or Fast Company. One of the key aspects of writing these stories is going to be the power of new. Now, when a lot of people do copywriting, particularly when they're beginning, it's all about positioning, benefits, features, value.

How do you create value for customers? But the art of conveying that with something that's new is going to give it a lot more media worthiness. Because if you think about newspapers, you think about CNN. It's really about what's new, what's flashy. And sometimes it's even about artificially making something seem new, even when it's not. So we see this all the time where old ideas are rebranded with new terms and suddenly everybody's excited about it, even though there's really nothing new about it. What's new about it is that it's becoming popular again because of the different phrasing so new ness is very important when you're doing storytelling and when you're doing copywriting.

And we know that from looking at the chapteric copywriter John Caples, he's always talking about how making something seem new is going to garner a lot of attention. We see that, for example, with Bang and Olufsen, when they're doing chapters on their newest audio premium speakers introducing Beosound Emerge. So introducing Beosound level this language around introducing, announcing, or new with an exclamation point. That's what energizes people and makes them want to pay attention to you instead of the crowd of competitors that could just as well get attention. So when you write news about, for example, a new product launch, most publications may not care.

So The New York Times is not going to care about your new widget. But within the very narrow niche that you're in, specialized publications might be very excited about that new thing you're introducing. Another thing that's very effective with storytelling is using concrete visuals rather than nuanced, sophisticated language. And we see this all the time in the political space on both sides of the spectrum in the United States. So, for example, Democrats have used this phrase over and over in the media as a soundbite, which is we're going to defend every inch of NATO territory. Now, they could just use a literal explanation saying we're going to protect articles blah, blah, blah, and defend every nation in NATO. But that isn't very concrete. It's more conceptual.

Instead, they're making it visual. They're making it tangible every inch of NATO territory. And that really solidifies the message in people's minds. Now, on the other end of the political spectrum, they use this word, we're going to build a wall. And immediately in your mind, you're thinking of this giant physical wall. But in both of these instances, really what they're trying to convey is something that's more conceptual, but using concrete terms to explain it. So, for example, building a wall really means we're going to get hard on immigration and protect every inch of NATO territory, basically means we're going to defend every country affiliated with NATO.

Politicians. People that are great at personal PR know this. They recognize people with very concrete visuals. And that's why, for example, politicians often want to invest in big infrastructure projects like a dam or a giant building because it gets attention and people don't forget things that are highly visual and tangible. We also see this with politicians in universities. They always want to build a new building. Now, despite that, a new building doesn't really help with education and that it takes a lot of time and a lot of resources. People that run universities know that if you build some big concrete symbol of your success, then people will remember you. So it's a very strong PR, Rick.

PR Storytelling 2

Another key aspect of effective storytelling is romanization. Now, I mentioned earlier in the Book that it is not really about substance. It's about performance. It's about putting on a show, not about really the underlying reality. So an example of this was I was at the Vancouver Olympics and there was a riot, but the media really wanted to dramatize this. They wanted to make it seem like the entire city was in utter chaos. Cars are being flipped over, windows are getting smashed. But when I was there again, this is just my own biased perspective of what was happening as it was really isolated events. Maybe there were 1 or 2 cars that got destroyed, but the media will use their camera angles, they'll use their language. They'll do everything in their capacity to make it overly dramatic, to emphasize things that are small and make them seem as big as possible.

A similar case happened when I went to a concert in Norway, and there were actually very few people in the concert. But when you look at the chapter recording of that concert being broadcasted, it looked like there were thousands of people in a giant stadium. But really it was a misrepresentation of what happened. They use certain wide angles. They use the darkness to kind of cover up where there weren't any people in the concert. So it was dramatized. Let's make it seem more exaggerated than it really was. And that's how you garner media attention. So let's look at some other examples. So there's the shampoo that was released that has real gold in it. Now. If you're selling shampoo, it's a pretty cheap product, so there really can't be that much gold in it.

And whether gold actually helps with your hair. Probably not. But by putting real gold in it, even if it's just a few tiny little drops of it or powders of it, it's enough to dramatize the message that this is about luxury. This shampoo is so luxurious that it has real gold in it, and that's the kind of thing that garners media attention. So think about you as a startup. Let's say that you're opening a Shopify brand for cosmetics or for shampoo. Well, is there some super premium thing you can put in it? Titanium gold, Maybe it has some sort of mineral that was mined by a famous celebrity, you know, some sort of thing that has a lot of storytelling ability, even if it really doesn't have any utility. What it does is it helps with the perception and it helps with you being able to get media attention.

Now let's look at another example. So out of shampoo, let's move into some hard electronics here. I was trying to research what some of the best speakers are, and I ran across this article that caught my attention. It's the seven best speakers, but it's not just the seven best speakers. It's the seven best speakers in the world. And there's an exclamation point here and it's 2023. So the dramatization here is that it's in the world. It's almost like the way a child would say something to make it seem so exciting. And that's the kind of dramatization that works. Now, another key way of getting media attention is using charity. So on the left here, we have Lacoste. And what are the costs? They released a series of polos with endangered animals embroidered on the shirts rather than using just the chapteric crocodile.

Now, there were very few of these that got released. I don't know how many. There were maybe a thousand total, 100 total, but it was very, very limited. So the sales of these were completely minor. It was probably even a loss for Lacoste. But really the gains are from the publicity. The publicity of Wow, Lacoste has swapped their logo with endangered species because they care so much about this cause. That's an excellent story. So again, it's performance, not substance. An even more famous example of this is Toms shoes, where I believe every time you buy a pair of shoes, they donate a pair of shoes to people in developing countries where they can't afford shoes. So that's a narrative.

And this is a case of a startup that's really built around PR. The key to their brand awareness was this whole feel good charity story and you can craft an entire startup around that kind of story. And the reason you can do that is because when you're so small, you can be so focused that you can build an entire marketing campaign just around that kind of charity narrative. Now, another key aspect of storytelling with PR is anecdotes. Now, when you're in school and you're studying research or studying science, often what we're told, especially in statistics, is let's get rid of the outliers. Let's not focus on the anecdotes, because anecdotes kind of don't matter that much.

What we're trying to look at is the normal distribution and what causes what effects. In fact, the vast majority of cases. But that's not really true with PR. Often what happens with the media is the media loves anecdotes. They love those minority stories that really don't represent the reality of what's going on. And that's the scary part about the media, really, is they're able to take a minor problem and make it seem like it's a huge epidemic. So I want to give you a specific example of this. I was doing some research of mine to figure out why Canada's food guide focuses so much on dairy? We have this huge category that's just about dairy products and thought it was very bizarre because dairy is usually something that babies in the entire mammal group, it's what babies eat and then they advance into other foods.

And also a considerable portion of the population is allergic to milk. So I found it very bizarre. And when I did my investigation, I realized that it was really corruption. If you look at one of the major councils that determines the food guide for Canada nationally, the president was also the president of the Dairy Federation. So a clear case of corruption where the government is advising people to eat things that are really trying to promote things economically for specific industries, special interest groups, rather than what's healthy for most people in the country. Now, when I presented this to a journalist in British Columbia, the journalist said, What would really help you with this story is not just talking about the corruption and the data and the research that you did, but having a story about somebody being negatively impacted by that.

So a good example of that would be somebody that suffered from a milk allergy and perhaps ended up in the hospital because they were always told since they were kids by the Canadian education system that they should drink milk. Now, that kind of anecdote is rare. So it's not really representative of the harm that's done by dairy, but it's the kind of thing that the media wants to hear, unfortunately. So you have to think about that when you're pitching stories. Let's pick some anecdotes, some stories about heroes or some David and Goliath messages, and let's focus on that rather than just the dry research which I was focusing on. Another key thing is you really want to pick up on trends because trends matter a lot.

Now, by nature, I'm a skeptic and I'm not really big on following trends. I think it's really just buzzwords and people are hopping on bandwagons that don't make much sense. So right now there's a lot of talk about AI. Now, I think it is a trend that really is impactful, that really is going to fundamentally increase efficiency in marketing and all different aspects of society. But a lot of trends aren't that way. But it doesn't matter because, again, it's about performance, not about substance. So what you want to find out is what trends are going to get attention because you can leverage that to get attention. The other thing is the supply demand dynamics. When a new trend pops up, there aren't a lot of people or not enough people talking about it because there's been a surge in demand for content around that trend.

So what you want to do is you want to research what trends there are. So one of the obvious ways is to go to Google Trends, for example, search Bluetooth. Speaker I see. Okay. Well, there's some trending things here, like loud. Speaker Wireless. Speaker JBL. You can also use YouTube. So I was talking to a YouTube expert who gets over 80 million views on some chapters and they were suggesting going to YouTube and doing some filters such as upload date of this month's chapter and looking at what types of content is really popular right now within the keyword that you searched for. And then what you can do is you can decide, okay, I'm going to publish more content around that, whether it's on YouTube or podcasts, it doesn't really matter. You're piggybacking off what's trending and that's going to help you skyrocket to popularity.

PR Storytelling 3

One of the easiest ways to get started with storytelling is to just do interviews to invite yourself or your CEO. If you're not the CEO, to be a guest speaker on a podcast, a YouTube or a television station or a blog, something like that. And one of the key chapters that I learned is that our interviews are basically fake. So when you're reading an interview on the news, it looks like the person is spontaneously being thrown a bunch of questions and then they just sort of intuitively and quickly know the answers to all those questions. But what I learned a long time ago from my brothers, because they had experience with PR before I did, they used to go on these tours where they would travel around the United States to do interviews with journalists, etcetera.

And what they told me was that really you and the interviewer are both colluding together to create a nice chapter. So what they're going to do is they're going to want you to know what questions are going to be thrown at you, at least generally, maybe not the exact question, but at least the general topics. And they want you to have an answer. They don't want you to have a lot of ums and ahs. They don't want a lot of awkward silence that needs to be edited out. So you're really working together with them to produce something. It's not just off the cuff. Random questions. So when I started doing interviews. So for example, with podcasts and YouTube channels, I realized this was the case.

You basically provide them with what it is you want to talk about, or they're going to tell you some of the key things, and then you work together to produce it. And often what they will do is they'll edit out a lot of the silence or awkwardness that's in the chapter to make it seem like a seamless production. So these are fabricated things.

These are not just natural conversations in most cases. Now some podcasts are going to be a little more off the cuff and casual and that's fine. There may not be a lot of editing there, but by and large, PR is going to be more fabricated. So what you can do is you can control the conversation, so you can tell the host what you want to talk about and what you don't want to talk about. So there might be key things about your company that are getting bad attention or that are deficient.

Just say these are no goes for you. And perhaps if they're leading the conversation, you can ask them what topics or questions beforehand and you can prepare for that. You can practice that before the interview happens. The other key thing is you want to have something to promote. So, for example, I was doing an interview before and they said, you know, is there something we can give away to the audience? And I gave away a free product marketing plan template, a one page template I've prepared in word. You could also give away a book, or it could be a sweepstakes where you say the first 50 people respond, get a free copy of the book, or it might be a discount or free trial, something like that. So the general theme is you don't want surprises.

So when you see people getting interviewed, they might look like masters, like they don't make any mistakes. But really, that's about controlling for surprises. Nobody generally likes surprises. Now it may seem like that because of birthdays and stuff. People like surprises. In the business world, it's generally a bad thing. That's a big chapter learned in business. So the other key thing is you want to make sure the host saves face. So if the host makes a mistake or they ask you a question that doesn't make sense, just go along with it and you don't want to embarrass them or make things awkward. You want things to be smooth. This is also a chapter that we learned from the book Free. Another key thing is you want to repeat yourself.

Don't expect people to understand what you said just because you said it once. Contrary to what you may have learned in school, redundancy is actually a good thing. Another good thing is to have notes, just like going into an interview for a job. Write down notes, Have those seven key things you want to mention in your interview, for example. You also want to use simple language. Don't try to intimidate or confuse the interviewer or the audience. Simple language, clear language. Sometimes it's good to use certain vernacular if your audience uses that. So, for example, appealing to audio files or engineers, you're going to want to use certain terms that make you seem like an insider. Another key trick is to avoid questions you can't answer. Now, I've listened to some excellent speakers.

So, for example, Byron Sharp is one of the biggest thought leaders in the marketing world. I've listened to experts on global issues and global hegemony, and one thing I noticed is they're very intelligent, they're very poised, but when they're asked a question they can't answer, They don't say, I don't know or I'll get to you. What they do cleverly is they answer. They ask themselves a question and answer that instead. So they avoid answering questions they can't answer. So that's what you can do as well. And that's often what politicians will do too, is basically do some sort of doublespeak or just answer the questions that they're prepared to answer. Now, another key note here from the book, Free, is that when you're doing something like television interviews, it isn't natural, it's not a natural conversation. So one thing is there's not much space for nuance.

You can't go into a lot of detail and say, Well, this is true in this case and not true in that case. And here are the details. It's more what he describes as a sledgehammer. And what that means is you need to repeat yourself and you need to really focus on one clear message. Now, later in this Book, we're going to talk about an article from metadata that talks about how having a strong brand voice often means having a strong point of view on a specific topic. Because when you're in the crowd of millions of messages in the world to stand out, often that means you need to have one clear message and that doesn't leave a lot of room for nuance. But it also requires that you do a lot of repetition to hammer home that point. Now we're going to talk about some tips that come from the book Fraction and within the book Fraction, which is a book focused on startup marketing.

We have some advice from Ryan Holiday. So the piece of advice here for PR is to pitch smaller publications first, because what gets published in smaller publications is often picked up by larger publications. So, for example, if you publish something in a subreddit or in Hacker News that might get picked up by TechCrunch, and when it's picked up by TechCrunch, then The New York Times is going to mine that to decide what they publish. So there's kind of a pyramid here and it's easier to get traction initially by starting small. So some examples of the best stories. And this comes from a chat with a Tech Crunch representative who gets pitched about 50 times per day. These are the kinds of stories that are most likely to be successful for you. We have a new product launch here.

Breaking a usage barrier. Now, a lot of these are going to be particular to the tech space, but there's certainly cases where you can modify these for non-tech startups raising money. PR stunt and just want to highlight a few that come from the book. Free PR Having Sspca puppies at a trade show booth would be a good example of a PR stunt. Another was when Canvas Pop gave away mock $50 bills at a trade show which were not real $50 bills, but what they were were $50 discounts at Canvas Pop. So a cool little thing to garner attention. A big partnership. So an example of this was when I was working in San Francisco for a series, a startup, and we landed a partnership with a much bigger company, which was Intuit, the maker of QuickBooks.

Uh, a special industry event that's coming up is going to be story worthy. And another key piece of advice here is to bundle one or more or two or more of these announcements into a big pitch because any individual, uh, thing here is not going to be as effective as combining them together. So an example here is we launched a new product and that new product breaks a usage barrier. So that's much more newsworthy than just one of these elements alone.

PR Storytelling 4

We'll continue with some tips from the book traction. And what we're going to do is we're going to summarize a successful pitch to TechCrunch. The pitch is short. It's to the point. It has clear contact information. It has links to a product demo and has a product giveaway. So the subject would, for example, be exclusive for launching pad press, dot, dot dot. So there are a few more details there about what Pad Press does. And in the body of the pitch email, you're going to say something like, We're going to give you free reign on an exclusive story about Pad Press.

And what Pad Press does is it makes any blog look and behave like a native iPad app. We're happy to do a giveaway to readers, and if this is exclusive, then that's going to garner more attention as well. You have links to the chapters and to other relevant information. You're not going to have a wall of text because journalists are getting bombarded all the time with solicitations. So you really need to save them some time. And what you want is a potential story that's going to elicit emotion. So there's something exciting, inspiring, or perhaps makes people angry because of corruption, something like that. There has to be some sort of emotion tied to it. Ideally. Another example would be a book that's written about Wall Street, and maybe it covers a variety of things.

But really what you need to do is choose some sort of angle, ideally one that is associated with an emotion. So an example presented in the book is that Wall Street is rigged, that there are certain high profile people that have an advantage in the stock market and you don't have that advantage. So that's something that is much more worthy that's going to make you stand out from all the other books about the stock market that are out there. So the kinds of things that you might want to think about is, am I saying something that's divisive? Or that has a strong point of view such that some people are going to approve and some people are going to disapprove about what I'm saying rather than just trying to appeal to everyone.

Because if you have an opinion or a point of view, then that's more likely to get attention to perhaps elicit debate. One of the key things to keep in mind when you're doing storytelling is you want to appeal not just to the journalists, to the journalist's audience. What are they looking for? Are they looking for business advice? Are they looking for purchase advice? Are they trying to make a decision about what to buy? What is their stage of awareness? Are they even familiar with the product category or if they are familiar with the product category, maybe they're just not familiar with your product. So make sure you're meeting that audience where they're at and you're using their terminology, etcetera. Now, I want to also say that storytelling can be used at various stages of the funnel.

So an example here at the top would be top of funnel content. So in my case, the top of the funnel is basically about promoting my personal brand. It's not about any one of my specific Books or specific books. It's just more, do people know my brand? And so what that does is promotes my top of funnel. It's not immediately going to lead to any sales, or at least it's not intending to, but it helps broaden my brand and can be done. Another example is researching award winning marketing consultants and you can see these lists of the top creative agencies. That helps with your brand, that helps with your top of funnel, but can also be used at the bottom of the funnel.

So for example, if I have high intent to purchase something, I might search for something like the best Bluetooth speaker and then I'm going to see lists from CNet of the best Bluetooth speakers for 2023. This is much more bottom of the funnel than just promoting my brand. Instead, what's being promoted is specific products, not just the brands at large. Another example here is the six best mechanical keyboards of 2023 coming from The New York Times. A third example we have is a high end speaker company and you can see that they're leveraging the credibility of these publications, Techradar and MoneyWeek, to help persuade people to make a purchase.

Hey, not only are we excellent, we're so excellent that these high profile publications are endorsing us. So these are examples of the bottom of the funnel. Another key aspect of PR that's going to help you, especially near the bottom of the funnel, perhaps in the middle of the funnel is getting into rankings and reviews. So a lot of marketing is really about perception management. And I would say that in business to consumer, it's even more true because often what happens in business to consumer products is the value comes a lot from perception, the perception, the placebo that sort of says, Oh, I'm listening to the speaker. Does it sound better? Does this product taste better? A lot of that is not objective. It's not about the quantity of sugar or the loudness.

It's really just about do I think that it feels better? And that's the value proposition. The value proposition has a lot to do with psychology. And one way that you influence people psychologically is by consistently ranking highly through third party endorsements. So I'm going to give you two examples of companies that I think do this really well, both of which create ergonomic chairs that help with your posture. So in the Philippines, the premium company that does this is called stance, very strong regional dominance here now in the United States and North America generally, we have another company that's springing up as basically a mid-range ergonomic chair brand and it's called Branch. Now neither of these companies had heard about it before.

I only heard about them because I was doing searches on Google, on YouTube for ergonomic chairs, and consistently certain brands started popping up. Branch started popping up in these rankings, and I had no affinity for this brand. I'd never heard of it, but when I started seeing it over and over in rankings, I started to think it's the best. Now, maybe there's some cheap company in China that makes products for a quarter of the price and are just as good, but the perception isn't as good. But it is when you're getting in these rankings. And similarly with stance, you can see I readed this YouTube chapter, Best Ergonomic Chair in the Philippines Part one, and they're comparing three different brands. And even though the influencer here doesn't endorse stance as the best option, he does say that it's basically the elite option if you can afford it, that's the best one to get.

He's actually recommending this other brand, this cheaper brand. But it helps establish the credibility of the brand just being featured in here. So you can also see this with not just chapters, but text articles here. NBC News, the six best ergonomic chairs, according to experts. So if you can get featured in something like this, that's very good. Bottom of funnel PR for you. That's going to translate very quickly to sales. Here's another example. Ten best ergonomic chairs in the Philippines, 2023. And we have the rankings. You want to get in these rankings, You want to get on those lists. You want to get those awards. That's going to convince people that your product is the best, that your brand is the best.

Public Relations Storytelling Examples

Want to walk you through a few examples of great storytelling for PR. Now, a lot of these examples are going to be from large brands, national or international brands. However, there are key chapters here that are definitely applicable for small businesses. So let's start first with this example on Facebook from Johnnie Walker. Now this is actually an advertisement, but there are aspects of this that make it very media useful in terms of PR and probably did garner a lot of attention. So there's a lot going on here. First, we have this concert. So the fact that we have a concert leveraging somebody who's famous means that it is both newsworthy and has wide applicability because celebrities have wide reach. Now, we have another thing going on here. Step into the metaverse.

So the metaverse is a big trend, a macro trend that's happening, kind of like AI. And that kind of trend is something we can piggyback off of for PR purposes. And we have another thing. We have a giveaway, a giveaway to win VIP access to the concert as well as VR headsets. So what Johnnie Walker is doing is they're basically taking a lot of PR juice, celebrity concert news trend giveaway, and they're throwing it all in the kitchen sink into one bundled PR pitch, which is also being amplified with advertisements. Now, I'm going to talk later when we talk about scaling the third of the three frameworks and how we use advertising to amplify. But before we do that, let's continue with some more stories here.

So we have this at core, an example from McDonald's, where McDonald's sends a letter and some free stuff to a hospital. Now, why would they do that? Does one customer in the hospital really matter that much to McDonald's, or is McDonald's really just that good that they want to do a great thing? Um, probably what they're thinking is a PR benefit. Assuming this is a genuine story. So this is a feel good story that's being spread through Quora, probably through Reddit and through the news as well about McDonald's contribution to the sick person. Now, I don't want to devalue this if it really was just pure intentions, but my point is that doing good and helping others is also something that can benefit you from a PR perspective.

So it's something that could work for your startup as well. Similarly, you can leverage what Johnnie Walker, an international brand, has done by piggybacking with an influencer, maybe a mid-tier influencer, if you can't afford a big one, and piggybacking off a major trend like the Metaverse or Bitcoin or something like that. All right. So another example, we have the Public Transit Authority in Vancouver, Canada, showing off this bus. That's super colorful and they're calling it a party bus. Now, something like this seems like a waste of money. Why would you create one bus that looks crazy? Well, because it generates a lot of PR, It's going to get a lot of attention. And that's the reason that you would do that.

Another example, we have a Shopify's PR here where they're talking about the Shopify mafia, where they're talking about specific entrepreneurs and how they launch their own companies. Now, this could have been just a boring story. Oh, how four people started e-commerce businesses. But instead they've created an angle. They've pitched it as this little branded thing, the Shopify Mafia. Now, an example like this, you're not Shopify, you're not WooCommerce. So it's hard to get that kind of attention. But what you could do is piggyback off Shopify brands. So if you're an ecommerce seller and you sell on Shopify, we'll work with Shopify's PR to get wider reach to get featured in Business Insider, you can be one of these people that they feature.

Even being featured in the Shopify blog itself might be enough for your small business and going with an angle like Shopify Mafia or some unique story about how you helped a little kid by selling your ecommerce product like that sort of stuff is just great for storytelling. All right. Another example we have here is Zellers. So Zellers is this old brand that was popular in the early 90s, maybe 80s, and this person got a Zellers tattoo, which is a very interesting story for PR attention. We've also heard stories about Harley Davidson and how people get it tattooed onto their skin. If you read the book by Byron Sharp called How Brands Grow, what we learn is that these crazy fanatics who do things like this really don't matter financially. So when Harley.

When Harley Davidson and Brand is associated with these hardcore bikers who are wearing hardcore leather, they're not highly educated. Maybe they're involved in some rough and tumble behavior. That's really not the customer base for Harley Davidson at large. But what these anecdotes are is great PR stories. It's really a PR play. It's not a marketing strategy. You're deciding who's the target audience. But with PR strategy, it's really about taking anecdotes and blowing them up in a lot of cases. And that's what's happening here with Zellers and Harley Davidson. You have extremists that are great for PR storytelling.

All right. Last example we have here is from a renowned Tim Hortons brand that's being featured in the Daily Hive Vancouver. And it's basically just a list, a ranking of their top donuts. So this kind of ranking that's going to consistently keep your brand top of mind and is also going to be controversial. So earlier we talked about how you should have a strong point of view and you should say something that is divisive or at least makes people reject what you're saying or support what you're saying. And in one of those would be a ranking of best to worst products or worst to best. 34. Dramatization

Examples One of the keys to success with PR is over-the-top dramatization similar to what you see in absurd soap operas. Consider Minute Maid orange juice below. Which message better hammers home the point that this has a lot of vitamin C: 100% or

200% vitamin C!   Consider how the CEO of ProfitWell did nothing but repeat the word "churn" over and over and over in a chapter to hammer home the point that he and his company help with customer churn. At first this seems like a complete waste of time for a CEO, until you factor in: (a) PR (b) word of mouth and (c) how it's easier to stand out in a crowded content market with a single, focused message.

Later I will discuss how customer satisfaction is one key to unconventional public relations. I suggest considering over-the-top warranties. E.g., instead of "lifetime warranty" you could offer a warranty that gets passed to your children, even after your death!

Such a dramatic offer could garner media attention and get tied in with news around inherited wealth taxes.

My client for one project is an absolute master of leveraging PR for her personal brand. Note the 140% below:

Note how he piggybacks off the news of Russia with this:

Or how he leverages the cryptocurrency trend with this:

PR Crisis Management

There's a critical mistake that a lot of startups make when it comes to crisis management with PR, and what it is, is they assume that the biggest risk that they're facing is a legal risk. So what the founder of the company will do, what the C-suite will do is they'll turn to counsel. They'll turn to their lawyer and ask them what to do. And typically, the legal response is basically to absolve yourself of all responsibility. We're not to blame. We didn't intend to do this. Our partner did it. Our customer did it. Whoever offload the blame on the government if you have to. The problem is that when you respond to a legal risk in that way, it can come across as insincere and doesn't necessarily validate the person that's hurt and the person that's hurt might be the customer, or it could be the employees, or it could be partners.

So you have to assess what the real risk is and often what it is. It's actually a trust risk. You risk losing the trust of your customers or potential customers, because there was some sort of bad news that came out about a defective product, or they believe that you maliciously lied about what your product was capable of. Or maybe you said it was approved, but it wasn't actually approved. So often what you need to do to respond to a crisis is say, we lost trust in our customers. So what we're going to do is we're going to get the CEO on a chapter, in a blog post, in the news, to try to win back that trust. And often what that means is doing a product recall or giving people their money back, or just apologizing and taking ownership.

Now, that may expose you to more legal risk because you're taking responsibility and saying that you are to blame. However, risk is ultimately really a financial thing. What is in the best financial long term interest in the company, and the legal risk may not be the one that saves you the most money in the long run. Now, the other mistake is just not knowing who it is that is really the source of risk, because often what companies will do is they'll respond in a way where they throw their employees under the bus in order to save face with their customers. But often, if you're dealing with a professional service firm, for example, your employees might be your most valuable assets.

So responding to that risk to employee abandonment might be more important than addressing the risk from customers. So the key thing here is to understand and isolate what the real risk is. Respond to that risk. And don't assume that the legal response is the best response. And don't assume that the response your lawyer provides you is in the best interest of the company.

Profiting from Surprise

Marketing chapters from the book. POW! Right between the eyes. Profiting from the power of surprise. So that's really what this book is all about, is surprise. Now, one thing that happens when you start to become an advanced marketing person is you start to understand that it's not just about accurately conveying what the value proposition or positioning is for your product. It's not about just saying how you create superior value. It's really about how do you create an emotional connection so that people talk about your brand, and they remember your product. Basically, it's really about standing out because it's a very crowded marketplace, very, very difficult to get noticed and even more difficult to be remembered.

Now this book is written by the CEO just for laughs. It's a clear example of where surprise is very profitable. Oprah decided everybody gets a car in one of the filmings of one of her episodes. So here what we see is that this garnered a lot of attention and it generated tons of buzz through the media. Everybody's talking about how everyone on the set of Oprah won a Free car, and the media impact was worth about $5 million. So you see, there is a cascade effect that happens when you do things that are surprising. It's not just about the immediate audience that you have, it's about the cascade of getting other people talking about it and spreading the word through media channels. So, for example, Oprah's website had an 800% increase in traffic, and the Pontiac website had a 600% jump in traffic.

So that attention that you get from surprise is very profitable. Now, it may seem emotional, it may seem super creative, but financially it's worthwhile to invest in surprise. Another good example is will it blend? So this was a series of chapters published for the Blendtec blender, and basically they blended surprising things you would never put in a blender. For example, this one has 19 million views by blending an iPad in a food blender. Another good example. Kinder surprise, one of the most iconic candies out there, and it's all built around the element of you don't know what you're going to get. It could be any number of different toys that are locked inside. Now I'm going to read you a quick quote here. Don't try to sell me. Just make it easy for me to buy.

Don't make me feel that somehow it was forced on me. Don't. Not even for a millisecond, make me feel that the decision was yours and not mine. Now, this highlights one of the things that distinguishes junior marketing managers from senior ones, which is the idea that you can't really force people to do things. You can't just convince them to buy. What you do as a marketer is you work with their preconceived ideas and you nudge them in the right direction. So that's really what we're trying to do here. When we're using the element of surprise we're working with people's innate attraction towards things that are interesting. I encourage a somewhat anti marketing approach, one that sells by not selling.

Just give me enough eye popping, eyebrow raising info to make me want to come to you to buy. And this really gets to what a lot of marketing really is, the real metagame of marketing, which is how do you stand out and be memorable, not just how do you precisely communicate what the superior value is that you deliver? Good example of this is one of the ads I'm currently running on YouTube and here on Facebook and Instagram, which is the billion dollar digital marketing master. So I hired this actor who is saying some absurd, over-the-top statements like, I had 1,000,000% ROI and I got promoted faster than the CEO of Google. It's a very tongue in cheek ad, but I see that it has almost double the click through rate of what you would typically see with a Facebook ad.

And I'm not saying click through rates are the best for measuring the success of an ad, but it is one indicator. A better indicator is that people are going to remember this because it was bold. It was over the top. It was not a boring communication of what value is that I create. Another good example is out of Singapore. We have this. So these soda brands are anything and whatever. So a very clever, humorous way of describing what people want. What do you want? Whatever. Anything is fine. So it's a joke. You're using humor to get surprise. So one thing to keep in mind is that surprising things can't be predictable or expected. So usually when you go to a hotel, you might expect a complimentary drink that's a very common lemonade, something like that.

But DoubleTree did, which was purchased by Hilton when I went there. They give you a free cookie and the cookie is really good. It's like a warm, fresh cookie that stands out now. Over time, that may fade as other hotels start to copy it and it has less appeal, but in the meantime it is very successful. Another good example cited in the book is waiting in line, and then someone comes over and offers you a free chocolate. It stands out, you might talk about it, you might even publish it in a book. So you generate word of mouth through that. Another example is with the director of The Sixth Sense. Now, the Sixth Sense was a huge success, and largely because it had a surprise twist at the end of the movie.

But the director subsequently released a number of different movies following the same formula where there's this dramatic twist at the end and basically the element of surprise became predictable. And that's one of the reasons that his movies have not done as well over time as they did originally, when it was unexpected. So even surprise can become predictable and unsurprising, ironically. Another good example is Gillette. Gillette keeps adding more and more blades to their razors, and eventually it just doesn't matter anymore. There's diminishing returns there because people come to expect that there'll be more blades. Another good example is a number of banks that were giving away free iPods. Now I did that. I opened a bank account, got a free iPod. But once every bank starts to do that, it loses its luster.

It's not surprising. It's not really worth talking about anymore when everybody does it. Okay. So let's talk about some other elements where customer service or customer success and support can really help with warranties and guarantees and things like this. So Briggs and Riley is one of the most durable luggage brands out there. And I wanted to know what all the hype is about. So I recently bought one. I bought this item here. I think it came to around $1,000 Canadian or something. So not cheap, but you know, not as not as expensive as Rimowa. And it's well-made luggage. It doesn't stand out as particularly innovative. The material seems to be polycarbonate, which is a little bit more on the premium side of materials.

But looking at it, you know, there's nothing outstanding about it. But here's what's particularly outstanding, what really solidifies what the brand is, and what the product is about. Because durability is not something you can easily look at and identify. I don't know that this is going to last 20 years, but there's some indicators that help me determine that. And here's what it is. Briggs and Riley is the only luggage company that offers a lifetime guarantee, and the unlikely event that your bag needs to be repaired. We are here for you. It is as simple as that. Guarantee. Notice the registered trademark here means if your bag is ever broken or damaged, we will repair it free of charge. No proof of purchase needed, no questions asked.

I don't know about you, but I have never in my life ever run across a guarantee, a warranty where you weren't required to provide proof of purchase. Now, I had to do this recently with a luxury audio equipment from Bang and Olufsen, and not only did I need proof of purchase, but I needed a specific type of proof of purchase where my name is written on it. It had to be this commercial receipt. I couldn't just give them the receipt that the retailer had given me, so they're very strict about it. Briggs and Riley, you don't even need to prove you bought it. Basically, they're standing 100% behind their product. That is surprising. That is different. That is what makes this warranty and this brand worth talking about. And that's why when I go on the Reddit forums and I read things like buy it for life products that last forever, Briggs and Riley consistently comes out as the top one to buy.

Whereas some other brands like Monos seem to be inflating their reviews with products that break the first time you use it on a flight. All right, let's look at another example, Zappos. Zappos offers free four day delivery. That's pretty good, but most of the time it delivers the next day, a surprise that leaves a lasting impression on customers. You said four days, but I got them the next morning. So exceeding expectations. Here is another way of generating word of mouth, of generating surprise. So you see how customer service standing by your customers and your products helps generate word of mouth. So it's really a marketing play, not necessarily just a customer support play. Perhaps the epitome of excellent PR would be Sir Richard Branson.

He's just an absolute magnet for media attention and he does this really surprising thing. So these stunts where he dresses up as an astronaut or he does some sort of extreme sport, like jumping from a building or in this case, he drives a tank down Fifth Avenue to launch Virgin Cola. Now you might think, okay, well, he built his whole brand on being bold, but what about conservative organizations? What about my company? What about a large company? What about a company that's just been around for 100 years, and the owner doesn't want to do anything differently? Well, even Harvard Business School. And it would be hard to think of anything more conservative than this than perhaps a church.

They decided to go with something bold. They even changed their coat of arms for a marketing campaign that resembles something that would come out of Apple. Another good example is Lakehead University in Canada. They put out this campaign mocking President George Bush. Yale Schmale basically, what they're saying here is just because you went to an Ivy League school doesn't mean you're smart, but being smart means you choose Lakehead University. So really bold out of the box thinking here with this, this kind of marketing and what I would implore you to do, especially if you're in a small business, is you can be really bold, you can take huge risks because you have no reputation to lose. And if you fail, nobody's going to remember you.

So perhaps the insurmountable challenge as a small business is just getting noticed and doing things like this can really help you. We also have Wilkie's University here. They created a series of ads calling out students' names as high school students in a bold, interesting play. They invested $120,000, but they generated, according to the book, about 100 times that in value. So again, it's not just about direct advertising or the direct impact of advertising, but it's word of mouth. It's the cascade effect that you're really investing in. And that's what really comes from creative marketing. Like these. All right. Now, Brigade theater did some really bold stunts to generate word of mouth.

To generate surprise, they held a book signing from someone, an author who was dead for over a century. They did a stunt where they brought entire desktop computers to Starbucks and got people to work on them as though they were laptops, so that's kind of cool.

That stands out, that's funny, that's nostalgic. And then they also held a fake U2 concert in Manhattan. Now we have four rules for word of mouth from Andy Sernovitz from the book. So number one is to be interesting. Nobody talks about boring companies and think this is one of the things for people like me who went the MBA route for marketing. And the more analytical side where you're looking at the numbers and stuff, we tend to think in very precise terms of, here's the benefit you're going to talk about, here's what you're going to get.

And a lot of direct response marketing people are the same way. But really you need to not be boring. You need to stand out. You need to be creative. You need to think a little bit more like an advertising artist to get noticed. And the other thing is to make people happy. So for example, the cookies at DoubleTree made me happy and it's actually a joke or a surprise built into this, which is that there are four rules. That's enough. All you really need are the first two. So that's one thing that makes his four rules memorable is that there's actually only two of them. So how do you put surprise in your marketing? You got to give them what they don't expect when they least expect it. Tell you. Stand out. And being fresh is better, but more difficult than being new. Being fresh requires that you always work in a single context.

What the brand actually stands for. So this is one of the challenges in brand management is, yeah, you have to come up with new innovative things, but you also need to tie it into the brand world, tie it into a connection and association with your brand. Like if Coke suddenly decided to change their logo, well, that's maybe not the best move because people might associate it with Pepsi or something else. And this point is also highlighted in the book How Brands Grow, which is that old ads, old marketing brand assets repeated over and over and over, is how you affect memory structures, which is one of the primary goals of marketing.

So the real challenge is the subtlety of how do we make this new and interesting without completely getting around what our brand stands for and what makes our brand iconic and distinctive? You see the same thing in entertainment, for example. People really just want the same old romance stories, the same old action stories, just with a fresh little twist to it. Maybe there's something a little bit different. Maybe it's set in a country you wouldn't normally see it in. Or maybe the character is a man when it's traditionally a woman. Just one little slight change. They want freshness. Not complete newness, not complete uniqueness either. The other thing is that people love free stuff, and free stuff is surprising because you usually have to pay for things.

An example of this was marketing the chapter game Donald Trump's real estate tycoon, and what they did to promote this was they gave away $1,001 bills, and they stamped advertisements right onto the bills themselves. So you can imagine the visual of throwing all these dollar bills into the sky and people running to collect it, and then reading what stamped on it, which is something that will fade over time but will basically promote this chapter game. And the PR stunt is one thing, but the media cascade from it is really where you get the benefit. When GameStop is publishing about the stunt that was pulled, more people are going to hear about the brand. And that's really where the real investment, the real metagame of marketing, is the media impact.

So not only do they love free stuff, but they also love being appreciated. So we're going to highlight an example here from bounce, the fabric softener company. An unexpected note was in the box. And within the box there was an envelope. And within the envelope there was a card that had this note in it. Dear friend, at bounce we believe even the little things should brighten your day. So on our 35th and 31st Canadian anniversaries, we'd simply like to thank you for choosing bounce. Thank you everyone at bounce. So there's really nothing here. There's no coupon, there's nothing other than appreciation. But it was so unexpected. You don't usually get this from CPG companies. So it was something that people talked about.

So it's worth talking about. An example of this highlighted in the book is Madonna Inn in California. I believe it's Saint Louis Obispo, which is a place that I've been to. I used to live in the San Francisco Bay area, so this is a popular area to go for, you know, a staycation or a small vacation. And what makes this special and worth talking about is that every room is different. It's unique accommodations, individually themed guest rooms. So that little angle is something that makes it worth going to. Makes this Madonna Inn stand out relative to the other accommodations that are in the area. Because you don't, you don't really know what you're going to get. Are you going to get some specific theme that you didn't get last time? And just the whole story built around the uniqueness is going to generate media buzz. So it's worth talking about.

Here's another example. There is a sign like this in Canada where it says "Attention dog owners, please pick up after your dogs. Attention, dogs. Girls bark. Woof! Good dog. So this sign, this one sign might get noticed by x number of people per day. But when the media picks up on it and when people start talking about it, you're amplified. The reach and reach is incredibly important in marketing. One of the most important KPIs. How many people noticed what you're talking about? So this message of cleaning up after your dogs spreads exponentially because of the cleverness of this. And one of the things highlighted in Red marketing, this was written by the people that did the marketing for Taco Bell, yum! Brands, KFC, etcetera is the idea that you're really investing in the ripple effect from throwing a stone into a pond.

So the ad or the campaign is the stone, but the word of mouth, the media attention, that's the ripples through the ocean. Another example, Nudie Jeans, says that you shouldn't wash your jeans for six months. Now that's kind of an absurd thing. Who's going to do that? Probably nobody. But that's something people talk about and people are going to reference it as, oh, you mean the jeans that you're not supposed to wash? Oh yeah. That's crazy. So you're generating what I have here in the visual is waves. You're generating waves of marketing attention. People notice tiny changes before they recognize massive shifts. So often surprise is really tactical. It's as tactical as a hotel giving away free cookies.

Does that have anything to do with the fundamental value proposition of having a place to sleep? Absolutely not. It's incredibly tactical. And because that's often what people notice, they notice the small things. An example of this was in a restaurant. They had framed images, paintings of cutlery mislabeled so they would have this fork and write the word spoon on it. That's something people talk about and take notice of. You want to be story worthy. So, for example, the Humane Society and SPCA released 120 Mad Dogs into a mall. Now, they weren't really living dogs. They were live life sized cutouts of dogs. So basically cardboard. Now you could have just put up the cardboard things.

But if you pitch it as a story, oh, we released 120 Mad Dogs into a mall. That's something the journalists are going to love, and that's going to generate lots of free reach for your marketing campaign. All right. Other ways to be story worthy. You could charge $275 for a burger, and you don't even have to. Nobody has to actually pay for it. It's just the fact that you have it on the menu is worth talking about. And I think that's what a lot of marketers miss in marketing is that it's not just about generating value, it's generating word of mouth with things that are superficial. They don't have to be substantive. Another example you may have heard of this quadruple bypass burger. It's absurd. It's crazy. It's over the top, but everybody talks about it.

And then ultimately, at the end of the day, you're just going to be selling your $15 burger. But it doesn't matter. The point is, the word of mouth got the attention. All right. Another example bare naked went door to door giving away food during Halloween instead of trick or treating and asking for stuff. That kind of thing stands out. That kind of thing is media juice. Why? Because it's timely media love. When things are timely, like built around Halloween or recent news or the holidays or something like that. Way more likely to publish something about you if it resonates with what people are interested in that time of year. And it's not just traditional media, but it's also going to spread through social media as well. Now be weird or funny. Okay. Don't be afraid to do this.

Shreddies, for example, these little square wheat cereals marketed themselves as New Diamond Shreddies, and all they did was they took the square shreddy and put it on an angle. Absurd. Crazy. Funny. Weird. Voodoo donuts. Very popular. Lots of line ups for this. And they did something crazy. They made an actual voodoo doll donut that you stabbed with pretzel sticks. Completely crazy over the top. Very distinctive. It's a crazy name. What does voodoo have to do with donuts? Nothing. It's a crazy name that people remember. And then you create a voodoo doll out of a donut, and it's. It's even more juice to talk about. Another example. Pizza cones. Putting a pizza in a cone. Crazy idea. Like ice cream, but it works. Do things out of context. So, for example, serve coffee in the elevator instead of in the lobby. Serve Coke like you would champagne.

Put a list of ingredients on your shoe box, even though you would normally only see that with food. Print your ad upside down the way you did or you're a luxury brand. Make these absurd ads for your jewelry where you have these beautiful women doing completely absurd looks and they look like they're trying to be funny, but you're actually trying to sell something super expensive that's going to help you stand out in a market where everybody's doing the same thing.

Advice from the YouTube Formula

Invest in bold, creative ideas that have strong viral potential. So, for example, there is this chapter advertisement for Squatty Potty that features a prince and a unicorn that is pooping. Very hilarious concept, very attention grabbing with a lot of virality. And basically what this did was it took Squatty Potty from a couple of million dollars in revenue to $28 million from a single campaign. You can see here that Squatty Potty has 50,000 subscribers. This particular chapter has generated 40 million views. And what it generated was a lot of comments, a lot of tagging and a lot of sharing. So this big, bold bet really paid off. And that's the kind of thing that you'd like to achieve with YouTube.

So this is consistent with the research that we have from Harvard Business School in the book blockbusters. We can see that for success in entertainment, specifically, what you want to do is make big, bold bets. So it's not about throwing out 250 chapters and seeing which one is going to rise to the top or hoping that at it together they're going to generate a lot of views. It's more about let's focus on a few key concepts that could go huge, and that's the most profitable approach to portfolios when you're in entertainment. Now, not all of you operating on YouTube are going to be in entertainment. You might be in something like education. So your approach is going to be perhaps a little less aggressive in this regard.

But I still think it's worth pursuing this idea that by investing a lot in editing and concepts and screenwriting, you can come up with something that will go big and put you on the map. 38. Gong Example The former head of content strategy for Gong provides some excellent advice on building a memorable brand. His 1st recommendation is to have a clear, unique point of view. Such a perspective can help you stand out in a sea of content overload.

Think about the stance you can take to garner PR attention.

Examples: My product marketing slogan is "you either go big or go back to selling the services." This has PR power because it's bold and can spark debate among those who feel product marketing should focus on narrow targeting instead of mass marketing. One of the YouTubers I follow has the slogan "Go where you're treated best." HubSpot's POV was a crusade against outbound marketing. Gong supports sales advice with large-scale quantitative data instead of the more common anecdotes and opinions. Their point-of-view centers around research.

https://metadata.io/resources/blog/how-to-create-a-memorable-brand-and-grow-revenue-with-your-content-strategy/

My #1 Piece of Advice for PR & Event Content

I'm going to reveal my number one secret for getting publicity and for securing spots for public speaking engagements at major events, major associations, et cetera. Or even speaking engagements and podcasts might qualify for virtual events as well. But before I reveal that secret, I want to talk about some mistakes that people make when it comes to things like PR and events. And one of the key mistakes is it's too salesy. It's too much self promotion. Now, I think the opposite is true when we're talking about other content assets. So when we're doing things like paid ads, when we're doing things like White Papers, often people do the reverse. What they do is they talk at a high level. They're too journalistic, they're not salesy enough.

And I've demonstrated throughout this Book how you need to do self promotion. But when you're taking the PR angle or you're trying to get a free speaking engagement at an event, you can't take that salesy approach. You have to go with something that is going to be more appealing and more value for the customer or for the attendee than it is for you. So you need to have a little bit of a shift in thinking they're less self promotion. All right. Some other things that people do is they kind of approach PR from this. Let's just try a whole bunch of different things and see what grabs. And often those things are just not very appealing to journalists or to anybody that wants to publish that kind of content.

So the response rates tend to be very low and there's not a lot, a lot, a lot of success there. Now, one area where you might think you have something newsworthy is some high profile, some high profile person joins your company. So, for example, I was working at a company and we had one of the country managers for LinkedIn join and I thought, hey, this is a great opportunity for PR. And then I spoke to a PR expert in my industry. He's like, Nah, that happens all the time. Nobody cares. It's important to us, but not very important from a publication standpoint. And there are lots of cases like that where things are happening internally, your company.

But it's just not, it's not publishable. One thing that is publishable is if you get a funding round, so you raise a whole bunch of venture capital, you get tons of funding. That's the kind of thing you can get a lot of leverage out of with PR. But that's not my number one recommendation, my number one recommendation when it comes to PR and when it comes to events is to leverage the data that you have. You have data. You have access to information that other organizations and other people don't. And usually that's because of the customer base that you have and because you often have data related to your product that you're monitoring.

And if you can look at that data across, say even just 100 customers, maybe a few dozen, if you're just a professional service company, thousands, if you're fairly established, what you can do is you can start doing survey research, you can start looking at behavioral metrics, you can start looking at spend behavior, transaction behavior, any useful, data based information. That's based on quantitative, measurable things. Is something publishable both from a PR standpoint and from a, hey, let's secure a speaking engagement standpoint? So I'm going to show you one example of that, where I worked on this at a company called Web Agility. And what we came up with was this speech that the CEO is going to give on proven recipes for scaling to 10 million to speak in front of some of the the most successful Amazon sellers.

And you can see that there's specific, quantifiable things here that are based on empirical research and based on outcomes. So here the stories and learn from the strategies of sellers who grew revenue to 10 million and beyond. Amazon insider Parag Magnani reveals the secrets of success after working with over 10,000 ecommerce companies. So we're looking at insights based on a large spectrum of a large sample size over 18 years, backed by data and colorful anecdotes. So data, the quantifiable aspect of data is important, but if you don't have that, you can also rely on anecdotes and qualitative data, which could be, for example, just feedback from interviews that you do with your customers.

You'll walk away with actionable insights to help you grow your top line ideal for CEOs, CFOs and e-commerce managers and multichannel retailers and brands with annual revenue between half $1,000,005 million. So here's an example where what the company is doing is taking all the insights that they've learned and data that they have on actual customers and translating it into something that can be delivered in the form of a presentation that the audience will find useful. 40. Personal Branding Public Relations A lot of PR is really about personal branding, typically for the CEO, but sometimes for an evangelist, mascot, or other representative.

Prototypical examples include Elon Musk and Richard Branson, but startup CEOs can build their personal brand by having a highly focused message to break through the clutter.

Consider... Dr. Augustine Fou (Fou Analytics) who publishes content almost exclusively on the topic of ad fraud. ProfitWell CEO Patrick Campbell published a chapter where all he says is "churn." Refine Labs founder Chris Walker repeated himself on the matter of "dark social" and faulty attribution A.J. Wilcox' reputation as a LinkedIn ads expert (not even for LinkedIn marketing, but specifically advertising) Here you can see that Wes Bush is known as the PLG (Product Led Growth) expert:

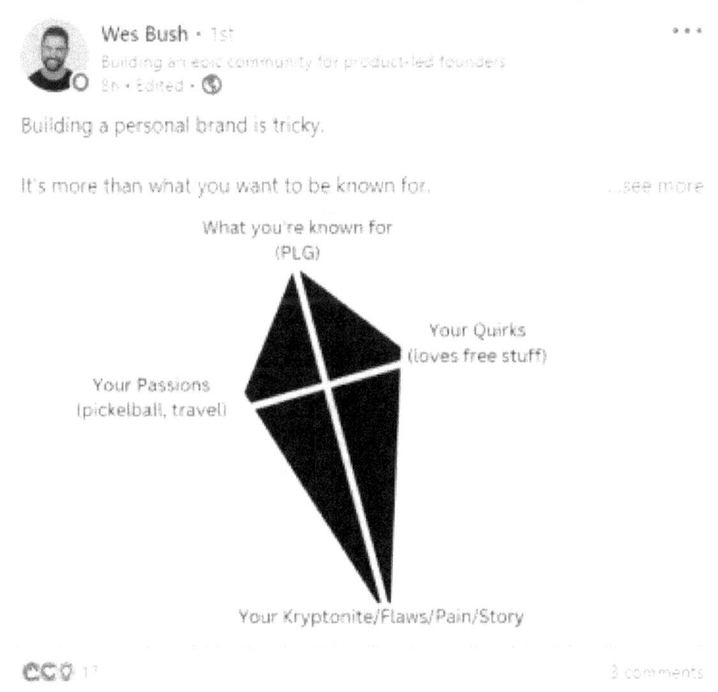

It's easier to build a reputation and get interviews when you position your CEO as the authority on a narrow topic of interest. As you scale, you'll need to add more topics of interest.

Startups typically need a narrow focus to break through and get noticed! 41. Public Relations Examples (Storytelling) Below is an example of how performance beats substance in the PR world. Nobody seriously thinks an 18-year-old could become the CEO of Disney, yet that's the premise of this story. The goal here is spectacle, not substance.

facebook  

The Wall Street Journal
Sponsored ·

Disney CEO Robert Iger has said his top priority is finding his replacement within two years. An 18-year-old Disney superfan thinks … See more

wsj.com

Could Disney's Next CEO Be This 18-Year-Old Superfan?

Learn more

 124   18 comments · 5 shares

Below is an example of how focusing on a singular message can help you break through the clutter to be remembered.

Below is an example of how to leverage publications to support a new product

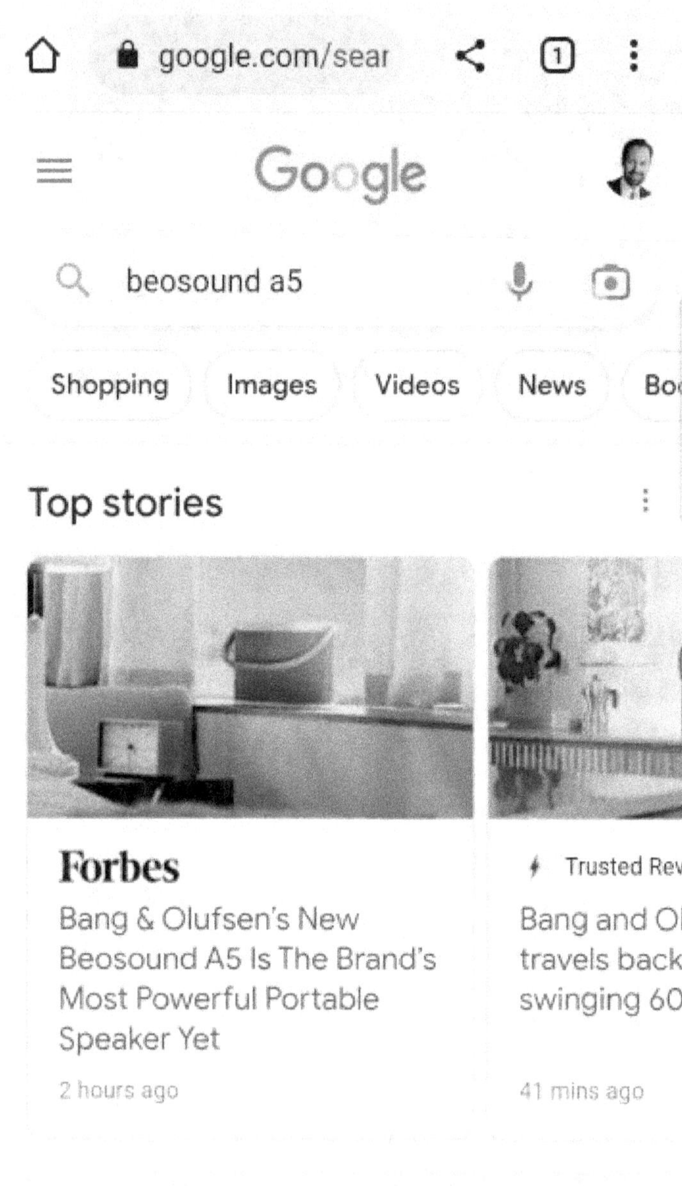
google.com/sear
Google
beosound a5
Shopping   Images   Videos   News   Boc
Top stories
Forbes
Bang & Olufsen's New Beosound A5 Is The Brand's Most Powerful Portable Speaker Yet
2 hours ago
Trusted Rev
Bang and Ol
travels back
swinging 60
41 mins ago
Engadget
https://www.engadget.com › bang-a...
Bang & Olufsen's modular Beosound A5 portable speaker ...

Below is an example of piggybacking of a major trend (AI) with a dramatized story (bringing back the dead). Note how important it was to word the story in this dramatic—instead of literal—way.

The Wall Street Journal ✓
Sponsored · 🌐

Companies including Apple and Google are embracing AI-narrated audiobooks: "It's a wow moment."

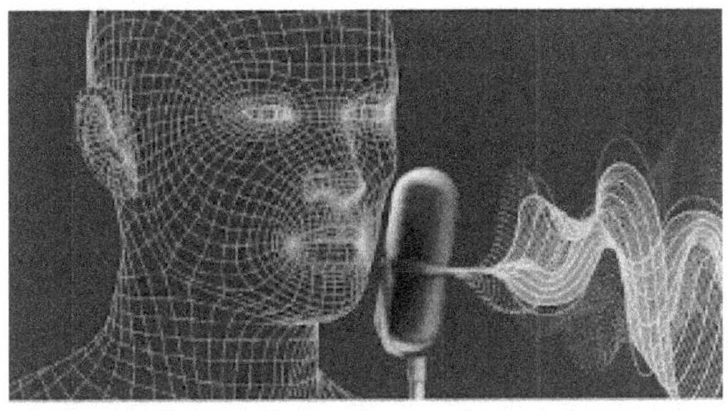

wsj.com
AI Is Bringing the Voice of the Dead Back to Narrate Your Audiobook

 You and 2.3K others   329 comments · 402 shares

Building a Story Brand

Here are some key chapters from the very well written book, Building a Story Brand. One of the key insights from this book is that your customer needs to be the hero of the story, not you. So this is what most companies do when they're crafting stories. They try to position their brand, their product themselves as the hero of the story who comes in to rescue the prospect, the customer. But in reality, the center of the universe for your customers is them. They're the protagonists. They're the ones who are getting up in the morning looking at themselves in the mirror. So really what you need to do is position yourself as the guide who's going to help them achieve the satisfying answer to the solution to their problems. Because their stories, the customer stories are much more important to them than your story.

So you need to talk a little bit less about yourself, take a little bit of a back seat and put the customer front and center as the protagonist. Another key mistake that people make is that their marketing is too complicated. There are so many details. There are so many pages on their website that people end up just drowning in the noise. So the quotation here is if you confuse, you lose. And people buy the products that they can understand the fastest. So what that means is you want to be simple. And you want to be predictable. You want things to be obvious. So, for example, when people are creating movies or shows, it's often very clear who the villain is.

They put on dramatic dark music. The villain is going to be wearing different colored clothing. It's very obvious that's what we want. We want people to know what to expect and we want it to be simple. It shouldn't be some surprising, confusing, vague experience that they have when they're hearing your story. So what you want to focus on is how your offer is going to help them survive and thrive and conquer their challenges. So to give an example of this, the. Painting industry is going to have these websites that are going to be very confusing. They're going to be ads talking about all these non-essential details about what the painter does. But you could simply have a picture of someone painting and just say, we paint all kinds of stuff. Get a quote.

Incredibly simple. So what this does is it just breaks through the noise. Instead of going through all the nuanced details about the different things that you paint, you can just say the very simple, uncomplicated message. We paint all kinds of stuff. Get a quote. So you're calling them to action after explaining what it is that you do. And that's really the essence of what these storytelling elements are going to do is craft a very simple message. Easy to understand message. And that's really the benefit of storytelling. So when we look at advertising strategy, there are different choices of what to do. You could tell a story, but that's really only one option in your arsenal.

Another option in your arsenal is just to say, here's the main benefit and here are the various features that prove that we're able to achieve that benefit. But what story does a really good job of taking complicated things and simplifying them down to a simple story? But if what you're selling is not that complicated, in my personal opinion, you may not need a story to sell it. So how do we simplify? Well, we do it through various elements of a narrative. So an example here that is going to fit a lot of stories is you have a hero. Who wants something needs to defeat someone. To avoid a tragic ending and achieve a wonderful ending. So you see how simple that is.

You're taking all the nuance out of it. You're taking all the details out of what you offer, and you're simplifying it down to the story.

And what you really need to do is remove anything that doesn't serve the plot because that's just noise. Now, in a moment, what I'm going to do is walk you through the framework from the book that goes into the detailed elements of what goes into storytelling. And this is called the Sb7 framework. So number one, you have a character who has a problem. Three. The character meets a guide. Who gives them a plan? And calls them to action that helps them avoid failure and ends in success. Okay, so let's go into a little more detail about what these various elements entail. So we have a character.

This is your customer. It's not you, It's not your brand. It's not your product. Character has a problem, and typically what you want to focus on is some sort of internal frustration, not an external issue. And meets a guy. So that's you. That's your brand, That's your product, that's your company who gives them a plan. So this is a clear path that takes away any confusion. And that plan is going to involve basically two things: an agreement and a process and calls them to action. So there are different types of calls to actions. There are direct ones and there are transitional ones. So a direct run, one might be something like a book, a demo of a free consultation, get a quote, that's the type of thing.

And then there's transitional, which would be something like a webinar or an eBook or a free guide that helps them avoid failure. So this is going to be the cost of not acting and ends in a success. So this is going to be how you're able to change the life of the character, of the hero of the story. So some key questions you want to ask is what is stopping your customers from getting what they want? I have some examples here from Shopify Plus where we're able to explain what the key challenges are. So one thing that's getting in your way is that legacy enterprise software is broken. There's something inherently wrong with it in the world of e-commerce or commerce in general is changing. It's time to change with it.

So another key question to ask is what will the hero's life look like if he gets what he wants? And so often in my copywriting, I like to reference Shopify because I think they do a very good job of storytelling. And what does this particular customer get at the end? Well, Jungalow improved conversion by 12%, sales by 61% and customer retention by 26.5%. Branding is basically simple, relevant messages that we can repeat over and over. So an example of where I'm doing this is something that is going to get ingrained in people's minds so that whenever there is a need for marketing, I, my personal brand immediately comes to mind. So to keep it simple, what we can do is we can apply the grunt test, which is like a caveman grunting how simple it is. So number one.

The first part of the ground test is what do you offer? Number two is how will it make my life better? And what do I need to do to buy it? So you could apply the grunt test for something like a landing page. Is it clear what you offer? Is it clear how this is going to make the prospect's life better? And is there some sort of clear next step or action to buy it? Another key thing is you need to stop using insider language. So this kind of vernacular confuses people. An example of this is in photography. Avoid terms like depth of field and instead simplify it down to take those pictures where the background is blurry. Very easy to understand for anybody.

Another key thing you want to embed in your stories is called The Story Gap. It's the gap between the character and what they want. This is going to really set you up for success because by demonstrating what's been separating customers from their desirable outcome, you're going to help be some the guy who helps them overcome that. So examples of this is I frequently talk in my marketing about how you're leaving money on the table by only having requests to demo ads. So for a lot of people, the only type of marketing they run is very aggressive attempts to get sales meetings and the only calls to action are going to be requesting a demo book time with me. So what I'm positioning the problem as is you're being too aggressive with your marketing and to be successful you need to focus on things that are not just these aggressive direct response sales pitches.

So there are basically three types of problems that customers face. And by talking about the different problems that customers face, you're going to generate more interest in your brand, in your products, in you. So the first is external problems, and this is usually what companies focus on. But internal problems are arguably more important in your marketing communications, but they're all important. So the first is external. So these are going to be things like having a leaky pipe, having termites, being hungry, needing a new car. But the underlying internal problems are going to be things like self-doubt and self-doubt, intimidated by technology.

And an example would be embarrassment about an ugly house. So if you realize that that's the internal problem people face, you could create an advertisement, an email, etcetera, that says something like paint that will make your neighbors jealous. So you're appealing to their internal problem, not just the external problem of needing to repaint their house. And by showcasing that level of deep empathy and the different layers of problems they face, you're more likely to get the sale than any old painter. And the third is philosophical problems. So this is something greater than you, something that provides deeper meanings, something like saving the environment, saving the world.

And we see that a lot of companies have been very successful catering to that philosophical level of problems. So, for example, Toms shoes, you're not just buying shoes, you're also providing charity for people that don't own shoes. Now, one of the key elements of the story is to have a villain. This is the root source of your problems. So an example of this might be something like high taxes, not frustration. So we want to get to the real root of what the problem is, which is the high taxes, not the symptom, which is the frustration that you're experiencing. And that's what the villain is. Now, something to keep in mind as you're thinking about the problems that your prospects face is that customers tend to buy solutions to internal problems, not necessarily the external or philosophical ones.

Talking about those other problems is helpful, but it's not really what gets them to open their wallets. So let's walk through an example. So in Tesla, we have the villain gas guzzling, inferior technology. The external problem is you have a need for a car. Now the internal problem is wanting to be an early adopter of cool technology, and then you have the philosophical problem of helping the environment. So all of these are going to be drivers of what encourages people to buy a Tesla. But really it's the internal one. You want to have that cool all electric car. That's the most important one. And then these are also elements that go into the marketing, the fact that you just need transportation and the also the supporting justification that you're helping the environment, whether or not that's true in actuality. Now. In the story.

You're the guy. You're the person that is going to help them make sense of their problems. And you're going to offer encouragement and tools that are going to show them the way. And to prove that you are the guy that you're acceptable as, you're going to use certain things like testimonials, statistics, awards and logos, logos being like high profile clients or customers that have worked with you. And as the guide, you're going to call them to action. So it's not just talking about their problems, but it's also getting them to act. You need to get them motivated enough to take action. And with a lot of brands, they think that they're overselling, but they really aren't. And that's why it's important to repeat yourself over and over. So one thing that I'm very focused on in advertising, for example, is looking at the frequency of the ads.

Have I shown people the ads enough that it's actually getting inside their heads? So let's go through some examples of calls to action. Would be offering something like five things your website should include or providing the healthy body checklist. It could also be something like a free trial or test for a demo, that sort of thing. And the key thing that you want to do with these calls to action is position yourself as the guide or authority. And as the guide, you want to help customers avoid failure. So an example of this would be educating them on the fact that nearly 30% of all homes have evidence of termite infestation.

So by educating them, providing this type of information, you're able to say, Hey, if you don't act now, the termite infestation might get worse. So I'm going to help show you the way to overcome that. And ultimately what you're providing is a successful ending to the story. So an example of this is this book that I wrote called Become a Product Marketing Manager and earn over $100,000, a very clear, a very specific outcome that can be achieved by following me, the guy. So a good, successful ending is specific and clear. Another example of a product that I had a lot of success with was learning how to sell websites for $15,000 each. I wasn't just saying learn how to sell your websites for more money. I was very, very specific. By the end of this Book, you're going to learn you're going to be able to sell websites for $15,000.

And what you want to do is paint a compelling image of an achievable future. So that's what you want to think about when you're presenting your imagery. For example, is that conveying the future, the desirable outcome and another key word that you want to keep in mind is transformation. You really want to obsess about your customers' transformations. An example is we will make you a pro in the kitchen and once again become a product marketing manager.

Unconventional PR 1

What I recommend when you get started in PR is to start small. Try to do something like get featured on a list of the top products in your category by emailing the person that runs that webpage. But ultimately, what you're going to want to do when you start to scale up is get a very high return on investment in terms of publicity, in terms of reach, not necessarily in terms of profit. And the way that you're going to do that is partially from doing things like on conventional PR. So in the next few chapters, what I'm going to do is provide advice on conventional PR that comes from the book Fraction, which is a book on startup marketing. So let's go through some examples. Richard Branson, one of the world's most famous CEOs, does huge spectacles to announce new products. So, for example, at one launch event, he wore a spacesuit.

At another, he was seen driving a tank through the streets. Uber did a piece of unconventional PR with delivered kittens. Now, does doing something like delivering kittens make sense? Does that really generate enough profit for the company? Well, in isolation, no, these types of things don't. But when you calculate the financial value of the PR, of the media attention of the reach, then it makes a lot of sense. And there's a cascade effect there through word of mouth and through other media channels. Picking up on that story and talking about that story long into the future. So one of the advantages of doing conventional PR is that you have less competition.

Most people are going to be doing conventional PR, but how many people are willing to make big, bold bets on these odd types of stunts? So that's one of the key advantages you have as a startup, is you can make big, bold bets. You can take bigger risks than larger companies can. So that puts you in a less competitive space. And there are two types of unconventional. According to the author of Traction. The first is publicity stunts, which most of us are familiar with, and the other is customer appreciation. So these are things like contests or handwritten notes to customers. Now, there's this widely held myth in the marketing world that the path to growth is through existing customers, through stimulating loyalty, retaining customers.

But when we look at the evidence from the Ehrenberg-bass Institute, what we see as the key to growth is actually the opposite. It's a new customer acquisition. But the advantage of focusing on customer appreciation is not that it actually has a higher ROI than acquiring new customers. It's that it's the pathway to acquire new customers in that it can generate a lot of publicity, it can generate a lot of word of mouth, and that's really where the value is. It's not actually the customer retention, it's the new customer acquisition. Um, let's talk about some interesting examples of PR. So we look at the company half.com. What they did was they were trying to strategize how to get national attention. And what they did was temporarily rename a town to Half.com.

And then they compiled a story built around how they're creating jobs in a small town. Even if the number of jobs is just three. The story is interesting enough that it would get published, and they ended up getting 40 million plus impressions and getting acquired by eBay six months later. So you can see that investing in unconventional products can have much bigger cascade effects than doing conventional cold emails, advertising, etcetera. Another example at PayPal's annual developer conference, we had Wepay, a competitor of theirs, and what they did was they placed a £600 block of ice at the conference entrance. And basically this was a visceral, physical symbol of how PayPal was freezing customer's accounts and they were able to generate thousands of signups.

So again, a big, bold risk, which is something you as a startup can do because you have nothing to lose. Large companies have something to lose, so they're less likely to do these types of crazy things. Blendtec, a very creative company that generated a lot of buzz because they created these viral chapters called Will It Blend, where they'll have a blender and they'll shove things in there like an iPhone or a golf club to demonstrate how their products are extremely effective. The Shave Club also was able to skyrock their popularity by creating very interesting and bold chapters. Now let's deep dive a little bit on the customer appreciation front.

So one of the interesting things about this is that even if you don't get a lot of traction from your bet on customer appreciation stunts, it enhances word of mouth anyways because those customers are going to be so appreciative that they'll probably talk about what happened. So examples of this would be luggage tags that you send to people with handwritten notes and you send those to people as a reward for mentioning your product on Twitter as an example. So you might want to focus there on influencers or people that have a lot of followers. You can do things like giveaways. Handwritten notes are also something that you can purchase. So there are companies online that I found that will write handwritten notes for you, or you can do it yourself. You can hire contractors to do it.

One common pathway to virality or early tests with these things is to focus on redditors so you can make early redditors who are talking about your product feel very much appreciated. grasshopper.com does things like giving away Starbucks gift cards, giving away Skittles. Again, doing the handwritten notes. In fact, this is so effective for them that they have two full time employees whose entire job is essentially to delight customers in these over-the-top ways. Shopify is famous for a Build a Business competition with six figure prizes. So holding competitions are things that not only generate customer satisfaction but can also generate a lot of PR. Dropbox similarly has competitions with rewards through things like an online scavenger hunt. You can have Mother's Day events where you send flowers and chocolates to the winner or to the mother, the mother of the winner of that contest. Hipmunk did some publicity for customer appreciation, such as flying customers home for free.

Scaling Public Relations 1

The other s in the three s formula for startup is scaling. This is what you do when you've already had some momentum with your PR and now you're thinking about how to make a larger impact. How to scale it up. The overriding consideration here is the importance of reach. Reach is one of the most underrated metrics, but arguably the single most important metric when it comes to marketing, because everything depends on reach. If you want to get, say, 100 customers, that means you need to reach more than 100 customers. So the constraining factor is how many unique people you're able to expose your marketing to. And PR is one of the most powerful means of achieving that.

And where this is best demonstrated is in the book by the researcher Byron Sharpe, called How Brands Grow. And in this book he reveals the seven rules for brand growth. And you can see here the first one listed continuously reaches out to all buyers of the category.

Unconventional PR 2

Continuing with some more examples of unconventional from the book Traction, you could do something like give away chocolate grasshoppers to influencers. So ideally with start up marketing, your branding will center around some sort of mascot or object or animal. Research has shown that that's perhaps the most distinctive brand element that you can have, especially at the superficial level, as opposed to things like your logo, your color or your typeface. So one thing that you could do is you can create some sort of give away centered around that mascot. So something like a chocolate grasshopper bunny, you know, whatever animal represents your brand.

So when you're doing unconventional PR, it can have a very high ROI because you could get tons of ridiculous amounts of publicity from a $5,000 chapter or from just doing one event at one trade show, and that could have a huge cascade effect. But don't expect them to all be successful. Many are going to fail. And that's just the reality of how the entertainment business works. When successful companies want to create blockbuster movies, they don't know which ones are going to be successful. They have a general idea of what makes for a blockbuster movie, but they have a portfolio. So for every ten that they release, they expect at least one of them, for example, to be a huge hit and make up for the losses and the other. So that's the way I would think about conventional PR is to do a few and invest heavily in a few, but don't expect them all to be. Huge successes.

So one little trick that was mentioned in this book is creating a chapter and then mentioning in the chapter a specific publication that you think would be interested in publishing it. And what that does is it provides an incentive for them to read the chapter and be like, Hey, you know, we mentioned TechCrunch or whatever it is in there. We mentioned your blog. Let's see if you can find it in the chapter that'll pique their interest. The cool example of unconventional PR that was mentioned is to charge a fee which was largely unknown at the time. What they did was they hired a stuntman to drop to dress up as their mascot, as a bull to get people pumped about Charger VI at the South by Southwest Conference. And one thing that they did was the bull was driving a Corvette, going around energizing people.

It got so out of hand that eventually the mascot was kicked out of the event, a very expensive event to attend. But the fact that it was kicked out is, again, it's more story worthy. So all the drama centered around this was very good in terms of elevating the charge of high brand. So there are three basic targets that you want to take unconventionally according to the book, Traction. Number one is you want to do things that are big, cheap, fun and original. Things like competitive stunts and viral chapters. Um, and also just keep in mind, one of the advantages of being a startup is that you can be more original, you can take bigger risks. There's going to be a much more conservative political weight when you're trying to do these types of things in a big company. So don't look to large companies necessarily for ideas like this.

You want to look at when companies were very small because that's probably when they're more likely to be bold. Another target. Number two is to be awesome to your customers. Things like gifts, contests, and amazing customer support. Once again, it's not that the direct ROI is beneficial to focus on existing customers, to focus on retention. It's the publicity, the word of mouth potential that comes from this investment in terms of reaching new customers. That's really where the ROI is. And lastly, prepare for failure. So as I mentioned with the portfolio strategy, don't just invest heavily in one PR stunt, have a few make big, bold bets, but don't expect them all to pay off.

Scaling Public Relations 2

Public relations works very well with advertising. I just want to quickly demonstrate this. So what I did was I went into the LinkedIn campaign manager, which you can see here, and set up a mock campaign, and you can see that the audience for this campaign is people that have the job title journalist. You can see that one of the easiest ways to scale up your credibility is not necessarily advertising to all your customers or all your prospective customers, but advertise specifically to the people that control the media. Those are going to be the journalists, and you can make sure that you raise your brand awareness among that small group of people so that later when you solicit them, you'll have a much easier time getting noticed. Another thing is to amplify your PR by advertising to prospective customers. So a demonstration.

Here is an ad done through the Wall Street Journal essentially to promote the Oreo brand. Now, Oreo does a very good job with public relations with this. They've also shown some research from MIT, which seems a bit ridiculous, but it's something that people want to read and find interesting. And it has more credibility because it's coming through a third party, which is the Wall Street Journal, rather than directly from the Oreo brand management. Another key thing that you can use is a tool called whitelisting. So I'm just going to read you off what whitelisting is from this Google search. So Facebook whitelisting, also known as creator licensing, is the process whereby an influencer gives a brand limited advertising access or permission to use their Facebook account.

So what does this mean? You'll be able to run ads from your brand's ad account using the influencers handle? So in the earlier example, I demonstrated how Oreo is able to achieve more perceived honesty by leveraging the Wall Street Journal brand. Well, you can do the same thing by advertising through influencers who your target customers trust, advertise through their accounts, and have control yourself over how those ads go. Be able to see their analytics through a process known as whitelisting. Now, as you start to scale up your PR, you're not going to want to do everything yourself. So there are a couple of options available to you. One is to hire somebody and the other is to find a PR agency or a contractor.

Now, my recommendation here is that you hire somebody first and foremost who specializes in your industry. That's the first place I would start. There may be cases where that's not what you want to do because you want to do something bold and different compared to what your peers in the industry are doing. And that's fine. But I would start with first trying to find a specialist. So for example, there are specialists in Silicon Valley who do VR. I've worked with specialists in the chapter game industry. Generally, they're going to be a better use of your money because they already have contacts in specific magazines that are going to be impactful for your specific product or service. So when we're talking about scaling, a lot of this comes from leverage.

And how do you achieve leverage? Well, one way is to piggyback off larger partners. So a typical example of this is if you're shopping, if you're selling on Shopify as an e-commerce seller or you're selling on Amazon or one of these other big brands, you want to use that brand to help skyrocket your fame. So make a story about you as a top Shopify seller, pitch it to Shopify and then go and pitch it to another media outlet that'll give you more credibility. This company I work for called Rocket Lawyer, they announced a partnership with the Golden State Warriors, which is going to have a much bigger brand recognition, at least in the San Francisco Bay area. So they can piggyback off that. When you form big partnerships like this, that's newsworthy content in and of itself.

So you can have a press release centered around that partnership and then keep leveraging that partnership for future media placements. You can also piggyback off large events. So big industry events, big trends. So here I have a picture of a robot to depict artificial intelligence. I. You can use the fame that's coming from these trends and use that to elevate your own fame. And you can also piggyback off large brands. So things like, for example, sports teams or city names or countries, you know, working with patriotism, things like that. Another technical use case is to use this tool called lead enforce. And what lead enforce does is it gives you a lot of very advanced targeting methods through Facebook ads.

One of those is being able to target influencers, audiences, and their followers. So traditionally with influencer marketing, what you're doing is you're reaching out to the influencer and trying to get them to promote your product. But in this case, what you can do is bypass that negotiation altogether and just start advertising straight to the influencers followers without their permission. Another thing you can do is you can simply target the followers of specific publications such as TechCrunch, New York Times, ET cetera. All of this can be done with the tool called Lead Enforce. Another key to scaling is automation. So one of the automation tools that I use very frequently is called Lemlist.

What Lemlist does is it automates cold emails. Now when you're doing outreach to journalists or potentially to prospective customers as well, you can do that manually using things like Gmail or Outlook, but you can also automate it using Lemlist. Now, traditionally when people try to do cold email with tools like MailChimp, which really don't allow it and they don't allow using purchase lists, I should say, what you're going to run into is very, very low open rates and delivery rates. So when you use a dedicated tool for outreach such as Lemlist or Mailshake, or some of the more enterprise options like Salesloft, what you're going to find is the open rates are going to be over 50%.

So it's much more effective at outreach and you can automate it up to say, 200 emails per day. Put it on autopilot. Now, Lemlist also recently acquired another tool that I worked with called Tableau. And Tableau does it essentially allows you to be much more efficient and automatic with your LinkedIn management. So it's going to help you with things like having your LinkedIn content have a higher probability of going viral, dealing with a lot of the time consuming processes that are happening using AI to generate content so that it's automated. So this would be a great way to, for example, stay top of mind with journalists and send cold outreach through LinkedIn messages rather than just through email.

So some other things that you're going to want to do as you start to scale up is you're going to want to start to get estimates of reach to dictate where you're investing your time and your resources. So one tool, for example, I found here was called Listen notes. It was very hard for me to estimate the size of podcasts, but here, Listen Notes provides a listen score and a global rank so that you know, okay, this particular podcast is this influential. I already mentioned that Sparktoro is also going to give you the percentage of the audience as an estimate in terms of how many people you're reaching. You can use other things like investigating their social media accounts to see how much, how many followers. There is a word of caution, though.

When I was doing Twitter advertising and Twitter advertising to people's followers, a lot of them are essentially fake or paid followers. So you need to do some testing to make sure that you're not overly investing in influencers that artificially propped up their fame and paid for a million followers, for example, on something like Instagram. One way to do that is to use third parties that are a check on how many true followers they actually have. One of the biggest benefits of doing PR is really getting the backlinks, and the backlinks are going to prop up your SEO. So make sure that when you're releasing the articles that you include a link.

In most cases, if you're doing something like guest blogging, they're probably going to allow you to at least have one link and perhaps a giveaway. So make sure that that's an SEO beneficial for you. Another key thing is that once you get a story published or you get on TV, that is going to provide a very short term benefit in terms of your brand awareness and your fame. And that's great if you're releasing an entertainment product like a book or a chapter game or a movie, because most of your sales are going to be in that short period around the product launch. But for most products and services, your sales are going to be spread out more or less evenly throughout the year, perhaps with some seasonality, for example, with retail and Black Friday, Cyber Monday.

But generally the default should be you want your marketing spread out and spaced evenly throughout the year. So one of the things you should do is once your store gets published, you keep milking it. So you use it and you say, okay, well we got published here. So would you also be interested in publishing us? Or you already published a story about us. Here's another story that you may be interested in. So you keep kind of keeping the momentum going that way. The other thing is that it provides social proof. So you're on, for example, on Fox News or CNN. Then you can highlight that on your website and your sales process. ET cetera. So essentially what you need to do is share your story and keep retelling your story. Your story of being placed in the media becomes a story in and of itself.

So you're controlling the narrative and you're getting as much value as possible out of that placement. Now, as you start to scale up, you're also going to want to invest in some better tools so that you can do better interviews for things like podcasts, YouTube, television, etcetera. An example of my setup here is that I invested in the Shaw Mv7, which is one of the top of the line USB microphones, which is very easy to use. It also has some more advanced audio outlets if you want to use those. I invested in the Logitech brio, which is one of the highest end 4k webcams. Lighting is one of the single most important factors if you're going to be on camera. So I use the Logitech glow light, which you can change the setting from warm to cool, you can change the brightness. It's not necessary to invest in very expensive equipment.

So you could get a $50 microphone such as the Razer Mini. And the key thing to making it sound like a more professional mic is just to get it very close to your mouth. So if I was really concerned with the audio quality of this recording, I would play with my settings and make sure that the microphone was as close as possible to my mouth. 48. PR Stunt Case Study: Ikea Ikea put furniture outside a transit hub in Toronto with signs that said "steal me."

How to Become Famous in 2 Months

How do you become famous quickly? To answer that question, let's go all the way back to 1911, when the Mona Lisa quickly became the world's most famous piece of art. Yet for over 400 years, it remained largely unknown. The Mona Lisa's rise to stardom cannot be explained by its product quality, but rather by a simple metric that puts a ceiling on the success of any marketing campaign. That metric is reach. The Mona Lisa's theft sparked a media frenzy that exposed it suddenly to millions of people who had never before heard of it. In other words, the Mona Lisa is famous because news of it being stolen reached a lot of people. Too often people think fame is built gradually through a snowball or viral effect.

If that were the case, the Mona Lisa would have become famous, perhaps by viral transmission between art critics, artists and so on, until its name eventually precipitated it to the general masses. But that's not what happened. Instead, said, fame catapulted suddenly from news publishers who already had massive reach. If you want to become famous, the most important piece of the puzzle is figuring out how you're going to reach a lot of people. Today's influencers like Jordan Peterson, built their fame quickly by piggybacking off the reach of other people like podcaster Joe Rogan and, more importantly, the news host Cathy Newman. All too often I hear the dubious suggestion that you should simply publish more content.

This approach is doomed to fail because it doesn't solve the key challenge. How do I reach a lot of people? Below are some real answers to that question. Number one launch a Facebook advertising campaign with the brand awareness objective and optimize it for reach. This approach works with almost any social media advertising platform, but Facebook has the widest reach, so it's the most sensible place to start. Campaigns like these are the fastest and easiest ways to reach a lot of people because they operate on autopilot and can be launched within minutes.

Moreover, they don't cost a lot of money, just $5 a day or even less. Number two, collaborate with influential people, brands and companies. For example, you can use Sparktoro to identify key influencers in your niche and send them a direct mail package offering to be a guest on their podcast. Another approach is to simply pay those influencers to promote your brand. When I worked for Sony PlayStation, one of the brands I managed garnered the attention of the top YouTuber PewDiePie. His single chapter generated over 14 million views. Another approach is to simply target the influencers Followers using a tool such as leading force enforce. This completely circumvents the need for any direct influential connection with those influencers. You don't need any contracts.

You don't need any negotiations. Number three Focus on a few high potential pieces of content. Harvard Business School's Anita Elberse teaches us that you need to invest big to stand out from the competition. The spray and pray approach of generating lots of content just doesn't work very well in competitive environments. Despite what influencers like Gary Vaynerchuk may tell you, her advice is by Mister Beast himself, who points out that it's easier to get a lot of views from a single chapter than the cumulative views of many chapters. To quote Mr. Beast, it's much easier to get 5 million views on one chapter than 50,000 views on 100 chapters. This approach explains the success of ultra creative chapters such as the Pooping Pony ad from Squatty Potty. This is where your ice cream comes from, the creamy poop of a mistake.

Number four Appeal to broad audiences. Broad appeal is an essential element to growth, as pointed out by Coffee Zilla In his chapter, Mr. B's secret formula for going viral. Contrary to conventional wisdom around hyper targeting, research from Harvard and the Ehrenberg-bass Institute affirm the need for mass appeal. In other words, mass marketing getting famous has nothing to do with patiently grinding out content for years as you gradually build a following. The key is to focus on channels that will get you wide reach and investing heavily in blockbuster pieces of content that are worthy of distribution.

Word of Mouth 1

One of the single most important concepts in growth hacking is word of mouth marketing. Now, let's look at the approach that a lot of companies take with marketing, often they start with something such as Google advertising. The problem with Google advertising is that the payoff is usually linear. You pay two dollars to get one click, you get four dollars to get two clicks and so on, you never really get that exponential return. You never really get Veraldi. On the other hand, when you invest in word of mouth marketing, there are much larger economies of scale.

So when you invest in the fixed costs of producing a word of mouth asset or word of mouth generating campaign. You essentially are able to distribute that fixed cost across many, many users because those users or those customers or those influencers spread word to multiple people each. So this is really one of the key components of how you grow, how you get exponential return from your marketing. Now, for the rest of this initial chapter, I'm going to be relying heavily on research from McKinsey and Co. So a lot of what I'm going to be talking about are not original thoughts. Now, I'm going to simplify and rework some of the things that McKinsey talks about to make it easier to digest.

I'm also going to come up with specific examples from my experience in marketing. But by and large, what I'm going to be talking about is research from McKinsey on word of mouth. Now, I'm going to start by talking about some of the key concepts and drivers of word of mouth. So a little more of the theory and research. But at the end, I'm going to give very concrete, actionable advice on how you can stimulate word of mouth. So the really surprising thing is that very few companies actually focus on word of mouth. I'm going to explain why that's the case or why I think it's the case later on. But first, I want to say that this is very ironic because up to 50 percent of all purchases. The primary factor for those purchases is word of mouth, word of mouth is one of the single largest drivers of purchases.

Now, when you invest in word of mouth, you really have a two factor benefit. The first is simply that it is a large driver of purchases and it's going to give you that exponential effect that I talked about. But the second is that there's a lack of competition. So not only are you getting the benefit of word of mouth, it is just a technique that's effective. But you're also in a low supply, high demand. Channel. So the payoff is even higher than it otherwise would be if other companies were rational and invested more in worth now. So if you're not doing word of mouth marketing, you're probably leaving a lot of money on the table.

So now the key question is. Why are companies not focusing on word of mouth? And I think the explanation, by and large, is that there was a lot of pressure on marketers. To attribute everything. To measure everything, to know the immediate short term return on investment, on everything or the number of leads that are generated from marketing initiatives, so there's an inherent bias to focus on things that are measurable rather than those things that have the highest impact. And what I know from doing marketing for a long time is that. The things that have the highest impact, especially those that have the highest impact in the long term, are not very easy to measure.

And we're going to talk about what some of those things are later on, but understand this bias towards attribution and measurable forms of marketing is very strong and to some extent is irrational from a company perspective, but perhaps rational from a political perspective. So a marketer can easily justify his or her credibility to, for example, the finance department by being able to quantitatively show everything, even if that means leaving a lot of opportunities on the table that could produce a higher return on investment. So one of the key questions is when is word of mouth most important because we have different marketing? Channels, we have different marketing approaches, and some of them are more appropriate in some context than others.

And one of the first key scenarios where word of mouth is particularly important is when it's the first time that a person is buying a product. So once somebody is in the habit of buying a product, you don't really need to stimulate word of mouth. Like, I like Snickers bars. I don't need somebody to necessarily tell me about Snickers for me to go buy it. Yes, that may help. But if I habitually buy a Snickers every Friday as a treat to myself, word of mouth doesn't have that much. Now. If we think about growth hacking, often what we're doing is we're dealing with that first purchase of a product. It's a new product that's on the market or a product that is at a small scale or at a small stage.

A lot of people have not heard about it. We're talking about companies that perhaps don't have the budget or don't have the scale to do wide scale brand awareness TV ads. So growth hacking to a large extent fits this first category, first time somebody buying a product. And in some cases, it's not just the first time that they're buying your product, but it's the first time that they're buying in that category. And in some cases, not only is it the first time buying in a category, but the category itself is new. So growth hacking sometimes happens with categories that are created out of nothing. So this is very much the place of growth. Hacking word of mouth aligns almost perfectly with growth hacking scenarios.

OK, the second case is with expensive products. Which is a bit ironic, because if you think about who tends to focus more on word of mouth marketing, it's probably business to consumer marketers, because one reason may be that there's less pressure for attribution, less pressure to attribute everything to lead generation in the B2C space. There's more pressure to do that in the B2B space. But we can see here that word of mouth is more important when you're selling expensive products and expensive products tend to correlate with business to business. Of course, they're expensive consumer products such as houses and hiring a lawyer, buying a car. So word of mouth is going to be very important there.

But if you're just buying some sort of impulse item at the checkout, word of mouth may not be the ideal approach that you would take. So there are three major categories of word of mouth. The first and possibly the largest or the one that has the largest impact on the market right now is product experience. So someone's direct experience with the product. The second is traditional marketing. So things like advertising and then the last is word of mouth campaigns. So marketing initiatives that are specifically designed to generate word of mouth with intention. So we'll talk about the first category, which is product experience.

People are experiencing products all the time, they're using them, they're testing them, they're doing free trials, they're doing demos of products, and they don't often talk about those experiences. They don't talk about the products. When they do talk about a product is when the experience that they have deviates from what's expected. And usually it's deviation based on key variables, which you're going to talk about at the very end of the chapter. So, for example, when people lose their luggage because of an airline, they talk about that. People like to complain. So there's a negative word of mouth that's generated when you expect to get your luggage back and you don't. So there's a deviation from clear expectation.

We can see the example here of a guy who wrote a song about United Airlines losing his luggage. Or sorry, from damaging his guitar, which was his luggage. Now, the second category of word of mouth comes from traditional marketing, so this is doing things like launching TV campaigns and because the ad was funny or because it touched people or it stimulated people or it surprised people or moved people, they talked about it with their friends. So the initial driver of awareness is just chapteric traditional marketing, something like TV. Paid media, but often the impact from the word of mouth that's generated from traditional marketing actually has a bigger impact than the direct impact of the advertising.

So this creates situations where you will see ads that are often very creative, very shocking, and you might think, oh, that's absurd. Why don't they just talk about the benefits of the product or whatever? The key value proposition is that you're trying to get across, but often that's not what you see. Instead, what you see is the kind of thing that creative geniuses come up with. And if you're in the direct response marketing space where you're trying to attribute everything to offers and responses, and by now it's hard for you to grapple with an ad like this one for Burger King, where you're seeing a movie burger, why did they not just promote a coupon or come into Burger King today? It's because the real return on investment is not the initial advertisement. It's not a Super Bowl ad.

The return on investment is coming from the people talking about it. It's coming from the PR that is generated from the campaign. It's the shock value. That's the cascade effect. That's where you get the economies of scale that word of mouth creates. So in this example, Burger King is showing a moldy burger, which is shocking. If you go to Burger King, do enjoy a tasty dish. Why would you want to see a moldy burger? And the point they're trying to get across is that they're using. Natural ingredients and not artificial preservatives, and you can visually communicate that by showing something that molds, that goes bad, it doesn't have preservatives in it. And Of course, Burger King had lots of word of mouth generated from this kind of campaign.

And Burger King also did something else shocking. They posted this on Twitter and it said, women belong in the kitchen, which is shocking. People are going to be in an uproar about that. It's sexist. Of course, they're not trying to be sexist. They're trying to stimulate word of mouth by making this social media post. And really what they're saying is women are underrepresented in the kitchen and they're trying to get more women in the kitchen. Really, I think what they're trying to do is just generate word of mouth. But this is the stated purpose. It Is very interesting that companies are using marketing. As a means of stimulating word of mouth, even though it still requires some sort of investment either in advertising or just distribution through their social media channels, perhaps hiring a creative agency to come up with the concepts.

The third category of word of mouth is intentional campaigns that are designed to generate word of mouth and in most cases this is basically influencer marketing. Now, I'm going to talk a lot about influencer marketing in this Book. But typically when I use that word, a lot of people think. I'm just talking about Instagram celebrities, fashion socialites, influencers are sometimes those people, but in a lot of cases, it's just people that have the influence. It could be professionals, it could be leaders of organizations. It could be athletes. It really just depends on the context. And an example of this is Red Bull. So Red Bull may not always be able to identify who the specific influencers are in the market, but what it does is it sponsors events where they know the influencers will be.

So just to make that clear, they don't necessarily know the individuals that are going to be capable of spreading word of mouth and have influence in the market, but they know that whoever those individuals are will be at key events. So, for example, extreme sports events, cliff diving events, whoever is extreme enough to go to these events, there's a high probability that these are the people that are going to be doing tweets. They're going to be doing Facebook live. A lot of people are going to be following them. And in that sense, they're influencers who are going to distribute the message about rebels.

Now, intuitively, when you look at Red Bull sponsoring an event. And let's say that there are only one hundred people at the event, why would a global consumer brand with mass appeal? Sponsor an event with just one hundred two hundred people. Well, again, the Arawa is hidden, it's like Super Bowl ads, the real impact is not the awareness that you generate from the AP event, it's the cascade effect that you're trying to generate. It's influencing the influencers who then go out and influence the wider market. And that's one of the secrets to Red Bull success.

Word of Mouth Drivers

I talked about the three major categories of word of mouth. Now, what I'm going to talk about are the three major drivers of work now. So these are the causes, the first is the what, which is the message. The second is the who, which is the sender of that message. And the third is the environment where the discussion is happening. Let's start with the message. Here, I'm going to reveal some surprising findings by using quotations from McKinsey. Across most product categories, we found that the content of a message must address important product or service features if it is to influence consumer decisions and the mobile phone category, for example. Design is more important than battery life.

First thing here that you may find surprising is that they're saying that features. Our importance. A lot of the time, what you hear in marketing circles is that no, don't talk about features, talk about that. That's not always true. And that's the point that I'm always trying to convey in my Books and my books is that you should not always focus on defense. Features are often what people care about, and features are often what people talk about. The other important thing here is that the features that people care about the most or that matter are not necessarily the same ones that people are going to talk about their certain features that people tend to share but aren't necessarily the ones that people value.

So therein lies one of the differences between the value proposition, which is a strategic marketing concept, trying to figure out how you're creating value in the market. But then there's marketing communications, which is about how to talk about things like advertising campaigns, etc. And sometimes there's a disconnect. The thing that is contributing the most value is not necessarily the thing that is going to contribute the most value to your marketing communications. We're going to continue with the quote, in skincare, packaging and ingredients create more powerful word of mouth than do emotional messages about how a product makes people feel. This is very interesting. So here they're saying that these.

Tangible. Beecher's. Packaging and ingredients are actually more important from a word of mouth perspective than the feelings than these high level concepts, which is counterintuitive because a lot of people with marketing, no, no, let's level up. They assume that high level benefits matter more than functionality in feature level components of the product. Not necessarily true when you're trying to generate word of mouth. Marketers tend to build campaigns around emotional positioning. Yet we found that consumers actually tend to talk and generate buzz about functional messages.

And this is the overall point that I need to get across is that way too often with marketing, there is this default assumption that higher level benefits are superior to other benefits and other features or functional benefits, low level concrete things. That is not always true. It's not even true in cases like skin care, where you would think that your self-image has a lot to do with high level feelings, et cetera. No concrete functionality is grossly undervalued in marketing circles, and way too often in consumer spaces, people are talking too much about emotional benefits and in business to business marketing or talking about high level things such as you're going to get more profit, you're going to save money, you're going to grow.

The problem with talking about those things is that it's often too vague and undifferentiated. So if I say you're going to save money by using my. Well, who cares, because that's well, that's the very point of every business, the business product is going to be either saving money or making more money. The real zinger is how? Or with what special methodology or feature are you going to be able to do that? It's not clear to me. Then you're just communicating a vague message that I'll never show to anyone. So really, consider whether your campaign, your growth hacking should center around low level functionality versus high level fees.

Now, there are cases where talking about emotional things is effective. And we're going to talk about some research from Jonah Berger later about that. But it's by no means necessary in all cases. So the third driver of word of mouth is who's the person that's sending the message? And there are too many things that you're looking for when you're considering who the sender should be. The first is trust. Do your target. Prospective customers trust this person and the second is belief. Do they believe that she or he actually knows the product and they're not just faking? And I'm going to throw a few staff at you. I hope this isn't too overwhelming, but. We find that in general, about 10 percent of people are.

And they generate three times more word of mouth messages than the typical person does. And each message that they send has four times the impact on a purchase decision. I'm heavily biased towards influencers. I don't define them in the same way that a lot of people do with this sort of limited understanding of somebody that posts photos and Instagram. But the stats should communicate to you the importance of focusing on influencers. And I do not just mean this in consumer marketing. I also mean it in business to business marketing, because these are the people that people trust. These are the people that have competence.

And this is where you're probably going to get an exponential return on your marketing, because by focusing on just a narrow group of influential people, you're able to reach a much wider group with far greater efficiency than trying to distribute your message to them directly. Another key thing here is that only one percent of them are actually digital influencers. Now we're talking about the market where McKinsey is looking at tons of data. It may be different in your niche market, but in general, the shocking thing here is that we tend to think of influencers as these. Digital bloggers, bloggers, social media socialites, but in reality, most of the influence happening offline in general now in a lot of cases, if you have a limited budget, you may need to focus on online influence.

But when you're trying to generate a workable campaign, you really need to consider that offline component because there's a lot of conversations that you're just tracking or considering. So if we look at. Jonah Berger, professor at Wharton, very well respected marketing influencer, says most word of mouth is offline. And he shows some data here. So, for example, if we look at beverages, 10 percent of the conversation. Is happening all for one and only one percent. Happening online. So don't. Be misled into believing that there is only one way to generate word of mouth and there's only one approach to key influencers. There are much more creative channels that you can take that have to do with offline marketing.

Lastly, the final driver of word of mouth is the environment where the conversation is taking place. To quote Mackenzie, once again, typically messages passed within tight trusted networks have less reach but greater impact than those circulated through dispersed communities. It's the small, close knit network of trusted friends that has the real influence. Often with conventional marketing, we're focused on how do we get in front of the largest audience possible? How do we generate as much awareness as possible? But when we're focused on impact, so not just high level awareness, but.

Are we actually persuading people to do something that is really about focusing on those small groups now? I I believe in focusing on small groups that have disproportionate influence, so perhaps focusing your marketing on an organization that influences other organizations or on committees that influence the wider market, I think that can be a highly efficient approach to word of mouth marketing, because if those people trust each other and they talk about your product, they were going to distribute word to other people who trust that. Now, the other key thing is that the environment very often and arguably in most cases, is not actually an online environment. So it may not be that Facebook group. It may not be that YouTube channel.

It may not be those things that are salient, but perhaps not as impactful as other places that are more difficult to measure and more difficult to narrow down. And again, if we think about how companies ran into this problem in the first place of not investing enough in word of mouth, it's because they were obsessed with attribution. So I encourage you to take the leap of faith, take the courage to invest in. Those tight knit channels that are often offline that perhaps are more difficult to measure but have much higher impact, because that's where you're going to get exponential return on investment.

Tips to Generate Word of Mouth Growth Hacking

I talked about the three major categories of word of mouth, and talked about the three major drivers of word of mouth. Now I'm going to give you some very specific, actionable tips to go about generating word of mouth. One of those tips is encouraging people to share positive experiences. Now, there are some key ways that you can do this. One of the most important ones is with trigger events. So, for example, let's say that you go through your net promoter score data. And you're able to see that people have very high net promoter scores when they finish a document in your product. Or when they complete a transaction. Or after they have a conversation with free friends in your product. Whatever the trigger event is, that leads to high satisfaction.

And particularly one that exceeds expectations. In a good way. Those are the key events where you want to encourage people to share. So, for example, a lot of companies, what they'll do is they'll say there'll be a pop up saying something like. Do you love our product? Yes or no, why? And if you answer yes, then you'll be prompted to write a review or perhaps to share your experience on social media. And the sharing capabilities are super important because that means every given user on your product or every given customer. Anybody that has access to what you're selling becomes a marketing.

A potential marketing tool for you. If you're able to empower them with sharing capabilities and when you exceed people's expectations with certain trigger events, they do actually want to share. That's the great thing. You don't need to necessarily incentivize them now, incentivizing them can work, and in a lot of cases you give people a referral fee or a percentage of benefits or you give them free credits on your product. It's another way to encourage people to share. Another tip is to involve influencers and consumers in product development. So the traditional mindset is the waterfall mindset of let's plan everything, let's create the perfect product and launch it into the market.

Those days are over to a large extent, except in some cases perhaps with things like entertainment. But by and large, a lot of products these days are. Created and marketed with the concept of agile, so we're trying to get feedback from the market, we're trying to get input from people who are external to the company and they can help steer the ship in the right direction. So by getting people involved in the product development, they almost feel as though the product is theirs. It's like their baby and they're more likely to talk about it positively when it's something they help build. So some ways of doing this is giving early access.

You can give people participation in Betis, for example, you can invite people that are highly influential, like people that run Facebook groups or people that are presidents of associations, people that have vice president titles. And so on, you can invite them to your Betis, you can invite them to join an advisory committee and create an advisory committee from people, from external companies, external organizations, nonprofits, and say, hey, we want your input. We want you to make our product better. And they can get special credentials. They can get special badges. There's all sorts of things you can do to get them involved.

But essentially what you're doing is. You're getting buy-in from them, so they will talk about your product through word of mouth. You're also generating buzz when you actually do that official launch, be on early access and be on the beta. OK, now, moving from the BIOTA to the actual product launch, you want to invest heavily in this area and the reason for this is that word of mouth is strongest early in the life cycle. And in some industries this is obvious. So entertainment, for example, you invest very heavily in the product launch because most of your sales are going to come in. And those initial few weeks when you launch something like a movie.

But in other industries, it's maybe less apparent that product launches are super important. Now, if you invest heavily in a product launch, your chances of generating buzz are stronger because people, as they do with journalism, have excitement about things that are new and fresh. And that's an excuse for PR is an excuse to talk about things. It's essentially something that the news has figured out a long time ago. People love hearing things that are fresh. Speaking of fresh, one thing that you want to do is keep refreshing the product experience, don't launch and forget it. You want to keep updating it. And the more that you update it, you give people an excuse to talk about it.

So, for example, Cannava released this cool feature where you can be a talking head on your presentation within Cannava rather than needing to use some screen capture tool. I thought that was a cool feature, again, I'm talking about features, not benefits, and it was basically a refresh of the product. So I spread it. I posted a screenshot on LinkedIn because I thought, hey, that's cool. And I support Kambah. You want to allow user generated content? And there are different ways to do this, you can allow people you can give people access, which would be a more sophisticated version of this. You can allow people to comment.

You can have communities that are built up around your product or around perhaps the problem that you saw or the category they're in. There's all kinds of ways to create and empower people to create content. OK. Now, on the more traditional marketing front, you want to create campaigns and particularly in business to business, there's this bias towards very rational. Let's just talk about the benefits we'll focus on. The value proposition will be very clear, direct. But in terms of word of mouth, you want campaigns that are creative. So Cadbury, for example, had an ad campaign that was a gorilla drumming with Phil Collins music in the background, that's very creative.

It's not. Cadbury, Cadbury tastes great or. It's something to give to your kids so that they're not allowed anymore or something like that. No, it's this absurd idea of a gorilla on a drum set, which makes absolutely very little sense when we're talking about chocolate bars. Now, the other thing is interactive. So people are interacting with something. There's companies like Eion Interactive that provide interactive content, particularly in the business, the business space, rather than just being marketing where you're delivering a chapter or you're delivering a blog post that people need to consume that something they're participating in. Maybe they have to input values in a calculator or maybe they're using this HubSpot website grader.

These kinds of creative and interactive devices are more likely to generate word of mouth. They may seem like a waste of money and time initially because it's like, wow, why invest in this tool? We could just do a blog post in a quarter of the time. But as much as the blog post is guaranteed to get produced for that set budget, and that's that time is highly improbable that it's going to generate strong word of mouth. So with word of mouth, you kind of need to make bets on things that have the potential to go viral. Another tip, identify influencers. I am going to walk you through later how to identify the influencers using this tool called Spark Torro, which is a freemium product. I recommend it to everyone, so definitely check it out.

There's other ways to find influencers manually. I can go through those as well. But the key point is you want to isolate who that small group of people is that has disproportionate credibility in the target customer group they were going after. The other thing that you want to do is you do want to message your prospects or your current customers directly if you can. So if you have an email list, it costs nothing to send a message to those people to announce, for example, a new product feature or new product. SMX would be another example. A lot of platforms have their own internal messaging tools. Another thing they want to do is Spend a disproportionate amount of time on messages that you're delivering to people that are more likely to share. So if you have a lot of data showing that, hey, this person is most active on our forums or this person tends to write more reviews about a product or that they show a lot of activity that would predict word of mouth, then perhaps spend more time and then maybe give them some sort of special acknowledgement of who they are and their contribution to your community. Another thing is to get influencers to talk at events so you may identify that there are certain key events that have a lot of clout in the target customer group that you're participating in. So you could invite influencers to give talks about events and they don't have to talk alone.

It could also be with a representative from your company. So you're going to get a cascade effect. You have the news of the event. You have the people attending the event. You have the influencer who's probably going to broadcast it on other social media channels. So the math is not as simple as how many people are attending this event. And a lot of people criticize event marketing because they say all the people going there are just other salespeople or other companies too far away. That's true. So you do need to do some math on this. But the people at the events could be journalists. There could be other companies that you could partner with, which is another efficient way of generating exponential returns for your company.

And if the influencers are there and they're influencing other influencers, you are going to get a cascade effect. And, Of course, allowing user generated content. And in this case, that user generated content can be tied into the events and can be tied into the influencers and can also be associated with the creativity and interactivity that I mentioned. So, for example, if your influencer is doing a live event, what they may do is invite users to participate in a contest where they have to submit suggestions for your product. Or perhaps they need to post a photo of themselves at the event, or maybe they need to post themselves in front of their computer with Instagram live or Facebook live.

So there's all sorts of ways to generate cascade effects and build these tips within one another to generate some synergy and to generate growth hacking potentialities. OK, the last point I want to wrap up on with the word of mouth tips is make your product experience exceed expectations in ways that matter and are talked about. So the things that matter are the benefits or the components of the value proposition, the customer value proposition. So the things that the customers care about. In terms of the value that they're getting from your product, and it could be at the feature level, it's not necessarily the high level, as we talked about earlier. The other thing is that you're focusing on those features that people talk about.

So as much as somebody might care about the CPU in your laptop. They may not talk about as much as some flashy cool metal casing. Now, I'm going to use a quote from the specific example, so while battery life is a crucial driver of satisfaction for mobile handset consumers, they talk about it less than other product features, such as design and usability. To turn consumers into an effective marketing vehicle. Companies need to outperform on product and service attributes that have intrinsic worth about potential. So what we see here is that. Customers value battery life a lot. But they're actually talking about design and usability. So if you're trying to generate word of mouth, you need to focus on those things that are more likely to be discussed, not just things that are more likely to be valued.

Word of Mouth Growth Hacking Worksheet

I created this little worksheet in Microsoft Excel, and I'll provide it here in this Book. It's basically a brainstorming workbook to help you come up with ideas of how to grok Hack using some word of mouth factors. So we have the word of mouth factors on the left and you're going to be able to come up with ideas and brainstorming on the right. So the first thing is identifying features customers care about and we'll likely talk about. So you can add those features here. Then you want to figure out the message I want people talking about. So it's probably going to be centered around key features or attributes of your business or product.

Then what you probably want to do is come up with a list of influencers, you can use a tool like Spark Torero to identify who those influencers are, or maybe you could do a search on Amazon or YouTube. After doing that, you want to figure out who the senders are. I want to spread the message and a high probability it's going to be those key influencers that you identify next, identify the environments where you want people talking. So it could be a YouTube channel, Facebook channel. It could be major events and your industry could be at the kitchen table. Maybe it's at meetups. Meetup groups with highly influential people could be annual events for associations, could be live webinars or Facebook lives inside that.

Then you want to identify product events that should trigger sharing, so look at things like customer satisfaction scores for certain features that you offer, and then when people use those features or have a key accomplishment in your product, you can use that as a key event for people to share because they're at kind of a peak satisfaction where they're there's a deviation between what they expected and what they're actually getting. And usually that happens where you have the highest satisfaction or where you exceed expectations relative to competitors or the status quo. Next, you want to identify people to invite to a product development advisory group.

Maybe you'll call it something different. Maybe it's early access, maybe beta users. But regardless, figure out who it is that you want to invite to that. And maybe the key influencers or maybe just heavy users of your product or maybe it's people that have technical aptitude. Next, I would try to figure out the benefits advisory group. So maybe you're actually paying them for input or maybe they just get a badge, maybe they get special training or special designation. Sort that out. And again, it doesn't need to be finalized, it's just a brainstorming session to come up with some loose ideas and maybe by the end of the Book, you may have a more refined way of developing this.

So, for example, I'm going to teach you some hands-on experience on how to develop key influencers so you don't you don't need to fill out everything and you don't need to fill out everything now. Next, you want to figure out a product launch initiative. So what are some major things you can do centered around the product launch to help give it more momentum? So a PR push, for example, or maybe there's free cake or maybe a bunch of people are put into a sweepstakes to win something. And after the product launch, you also want to have like many launches to stimulate word of mouth. So think about product refresh initiatives or maybe your product 2.0 or when you launch the next feature in the mobile version of your product or something like that. All right.

Now, you want to think about user generated content ideas. Do you have a community form? Do you have a place where people submit ideas? Is there a YouTube channel that's super active or can people contribute to your blog or have discussions somewhere and tutorial chapters on using our product? You also want to come up with creative and interactive campaign ideas, so, for example, you can go to Ion Interactive, look at some of their interactive content ideas and maybe come up with your own. It could be a website greater than a calculator could be something that people participate in, like a contest where they have to submit ideas. Think about the messages that you can send to direct customers so people that are already in your database.

I would also try to figure out a tailored message to people that you think might be highly likely to generate word of mouth within that database. So perhaps people that are super users or people that communicate the most with their people or people that you know are famous and are using your product. Other presidents, president's associations, events to invite influencers to speak out and just look at major events in your industry or maybe just the most influential events, maybe they don't have a lot of people, but they have the most influential people at those events. Next, think about other user generated content that could be associated with those events. So a contest that's associated with that event or certain things that people do if they show up to your booth at that event.

I would also think about product experience, ideas in general, so one of the key drivers of word of mouth is just whether the product experience was exceptional or was it more than I expected? And then the next general category is traditional campaign ideas. So if you're already doing something like a TV ad or Google ads or LinkedIn ads, whatever traditional marketing is for you, think about those and think about ways that you can make them have more potential for word of mouth by being perhaps more creative and more interactive. And then lastly, general ideas on special word of mouth campaigns. It could be tied to events, could be tied to online forums, could be tied to meet up groups, could be just centered around perhaps a very respected person that happens to be a strong advocate for your product.

Canva Word of Mouth Growth Hacking Case Study

One of the best products to demonstrate word of mouth is Cannava, for those of you who don't know, Cannava is this incredible tool that's available for free. It's a cloud based system that you log into through a Web browser. And what you're able to do is create graphics extremely quickly and easily. So it's kind of like a substitute for Adobe Creative Suite, especially for people that may not be professional designers, but have a little bit of design aptitude. So how did Cannava become incredibly popular? Well, the first thing is that it's a great product, it delivers on the value proposition very well, and it solves a critical problem, which is that there are people in the market who want to create designs. They want to create a lot of designs.

And it's expensive to use products like Adobe Creative Suite. There is a high learning curve. There are tons of pain points that can be solved similar to Uber, which solved tons of problems that exist in the taxi market. But looking at it from a growth hacking perspective, rather than just the product features, we need to talk about how it stimulated word of mouth. So one of the most important things here is that the initial users that really drove the popularity of Cannava, were people that use the product very frequently and those were bloggers and social media marketers. And there are a couple of key advantages here.

Bloggers have followings, bloggers talk a lot, bloggers publish content, so naturally, if a blogger likes something, it's highly likely that they're going to talk about it. Social media, marketers, same thing. These are people that are in the business of marketing things. So if you give them something they like and they're using it all the time and they're super users, they're going to spread the word for you. And that's why Cannava really did not need to invest anything in paid advertising. Instead, just focus on those key users that have word of mouth potential. The second thing is that Kambah has features that are worth talking about. The number one feature is that it's incredibly easy to use, it's easy to use, it's fast. And the other thing is the product attribute is free. So Of course, you're going to share.

A product that's free to other people because then they can take advantage of it, too. And you're not just spreading word about something so you can get some affiliate commission. No, you're actually providing value to people without expecting anything in return. Now, I heard about this product through my brother because I was telling him about what my needs were. And I'm like, you know, as much as I'm familiar with Photoshop and Illustrator, et cetera, I really don't want to just buy that platform. It doesn't really serve my needs. He told me about it and he said it's free. So what they did was they used a freemium model, which is incredible.

When you have a large user base, it increases your top funnel tremendously. And they just had a lot of key features that were worth talking about because they were incredibly well executed. Now, the last factor here that was important for word of mouth is influencers. For example, we have a guy, Kawasaki, who started using Kantha. He wasn't solicited to do it. He just started using it. And then Cannava noticed. So they approached him and then they made him a chief evangelist. And according to at least one source, Guy Kawasaki helped Cannava on the road to double its user base. So three of the key things to drive word of mouth, those users that are highly likely to talk about your product, key features that are worth talking about, and then influencers who help cascade the message.

Viral Content Growth Hacking

Viral content sounds like a cheesy way to acquire customers, but it's actually quite credible. I'll walk you through how to approach this marketing technique. The approach many people take with content marketing is to create a calendar, constantly produce content. For example, a company might release 10 chapters, but each chapter might only generate around one hundred views, often a better use of your time to focus on one really high quality chapter that generates tens of thousands of views when this chapter goes viral. You'll have an exponential return on investment. Very few pieces of content generate a high number of shares, so you should focus on quality rather than quantity.

If the majority of shares and views skew towards a small handful of pieces of content, then focus on creating something with viral potential. A couple of examples are depicted on the right. One is a chapter of a molding burger. This shocking advertisement generates tons of. Similarly, the Will It Blend chapter series generated tons of buzz for its hilarious shock appeal. If morality doesn't just happen randomly, there's actually a science to creating viral content. You may already be familiar with this from the book Contagious by Wharton Professor Jonah Berger. Here are the six key principles that drive Rally one social currency.

In other words, people share things that make them seem smart and helpful, things that make them look better than their friends and colleagues to trigger people sharing things that they remember based on triggers. For example, the medicine Robitussin tried to associate the product with coughs. So every time people cough, they think of the Robitussin brand. The cough is the trigger emotion. People share emotional content. Consider, for example, creating a viral chapter based on the emotional journey of one of your customers from rags to riches. Public people share things that are public, the Apple logo, for example, appears on the outside of the laptop where other people see it as social proof of its quality.

Plug ins and add ons that carry a brand logo are more likely to get shared and spoken about. Practical value, useful things get shared. If your piece of content is educational and solves a problem, it is more likely to get shared LASLEY stories people think in terms of narratives. This is just how our minds operate. So if you can package your content into a story, it may go viral. For example, when you put a presentation on SlideShare, consider pitching it as a story rather than just a series of facts. Begin with the problem, the conflict and then the resolution. When you create viral content, you do not need to use all of these principles, focus on a handful that makes sense for your market.

Here are a few more examples to help you come up with viable ideas, an emotional, inspiring chapter that tells the story of one of your customers achieving his lifelong dream. A website ad that always displays your logo, a tip sheet that people want to share because it makes them seem smart and helpful. A humorous demonstration of your products benefits similar to Blendtec with Will it blend chapters? Another way to create viral content is to talk about extreme cases, for example, one of my most popular blog posts was the best accounting website I had ever seen. I didn't talk about a good website or a great website. Instead, I talked about the best website ever.

You can also do the opposite by talking about the absolute worst. One of the keys to success with viral content is tactical copywriting adjectives are particularly important in driving interest. They may seem superfluous at first, but they're actually important to stimulate curiosity and emotion. Here's a good example. I saw a promotion recently for an interview with DJ Abram. I never heard of this guy before, but what caught my attention was this line, the highest paid marketing consultant. I get the opportunity to listen to advice from the highest paid marketing consultant in the world. Wow, seems interesting. Now, this guy did an excellent job with positioning himself through copywriting.

Viral Word of Mouth in the Book Industry

What I'm going to do now is take a look at the book industry as a demonstration of word of mouth marketing. Now, as many of you may be aware, the book market is extremely competitive for a number of reasons. One of the main reasons is that there are low barriers to entry. You don't need a factory, huge capital outlay to be able to write a book. Anyone working in a basement or in a Starbucks can drum up a book. The second thing is that when you're selling entertainment and this is more true with fiction books, there is a lot of competition because. There are so many substitutes for books so one can choose to write a book, to read a book, or they can choose to read a movie or they can choose to play a chapter game.

So you are not just competing with other books, you're competing with other media that provide the entertainment. This man is giving a TED talk, and he was a literary agent for decades, and he's asking the question. What makes for a best seller? He has a collage of all these best sellers. And one of the hypotheses about what a best seller is, is that it's something unique, it's something groundbreaking that people want to talk about. And he dispels that idea by saying that actually a lot of successful books and what literary agents look for are things that are familiar. And we know from our clinical psychology that people do like things that are familiar to them.

So what then makes for a best seller, if it's not something that's unique and so much different from all the other books that are saturating the market, he says it really comes down to the reader finishing the book and talking about it. So it's really about word of mouth, the success of a book in terms of becoming a bestseller. Is its ability to generate word of mouth? When somebody finishes a book, there is a sense of satisfaction. There is a sense of pride. And if somebody actually finishes a book and doesn't just skim it, it doesn't just start. There was a high probability that they actually liked the book. So they're going to talk about it. And then when their friend hears about it, that friend is going to go read the book.

And then they were going to finish it and they were going to talk about it. So when you're selling a cheap product like a book, let's say the book is Ten Dollars and. A fraction of that is going to be the profit. It's actually very difficult to acquire that customer because you might spend, say, 20 dollars to acquire somebody to pay ten dollars and then let's say your profit is actually five dollars or seven dollars or something like that. So it's very difficult to rely on linear payoff types of marketing. It's much more efficient and you achieve much greater economies of scale. If you're able to create that snowball effect, that avalanche, that cascade that happens with word of mouth where you're a you're paying to broadcast the book to the initial group of people.

But then by investing in that initial group, you were able to get an explosion of growth from the word of mouth and the recommendations that span from that. So really, the key to success with becoming a best seller is the capacity of a book to generate word of mouth. And let's talk about why that's the case. Well, if we go back to the Steps framework from Jonah Berger, that's in the book Contagious. I would say that the single most important factor here is social currency. There is a pride or a sense that you're educated, you're well read, your perhaps higher status or you are able to provide value to people and that makes you look good. So there is social currency that is a benefit to somebody when they share a book that they finished. And there are all sorts of factors that go into that.

So with entertainment, it's more I'm going to share with you something that was exciting and that was cool and it's going to make me look cool. But with nonfiction, it's going to be more along the lines of, hey, this helped me solve this problem. You have that problem so let me help you. And that's one of the reasons that books become contagious is because of their capacity to generate social currency. Now, some of these other factors do play a role as well. But the last one is probably the most important, which is the idea of stories. And there's nothing that epitomizes stories more than a book itself. And that's one of the reasons that the top best sellers are often stories about things like revenge, which is a very emotional theme. And Of course, we see that nonfiction books don't actually sell as much as the best selling fiction books.

Because of a lot of psychological factors that are at play here. Now, what we're going to do is look at this man who is an international best selling Canadian author, and he's giving advice on what makes a book become a bestseller. And the key concept that he's talking about is breathability. So the books that have. Pictures in them, they have large fonts, they are easy to skim. And what he does is he opens the book and he says this is what a lot of people do in the Reevaluated book. They're just kind of flipping through random pages in the middle of the book. What they're assessing, he says, is the breathability of the book.

And what that means is how easy is it to digest? How easy is it going to be to actually finish this book? Now, sometimes very dense books, very thorough books do become big hits. But he's saying that by and large, it's these books that are easy to consume. Because what ends up happening is a lot of people are able to finish books, but when they do finish it, they talk about it. So a lot of these books that became bestsellers are finished books and finished books tend to be breathable, consumable things that are broken up into chapters rather than just being dense blocks of text like a text book might be. And you can see here, they don't like sharing books that they haven't got through.

So that is one of the keys to generating word of mouth with books is to make it so that people are actually able to finish it, then they're going to want to share it. Then it's going to generate social currency. A lot of success in terms of the word of mouth generated from non-fiction books comes from the practical value. So it's very concrete benefits about getting somebody from point A to point B, solving specific problems. Now, here is a non-fiction book that isn't centered around that practical value. It's called Everything Men Know About Women. And the funny thing about this book is that it's just a bunch of blank pages, so it's a big joke that men know nothing about women and that's why there's nothing in this book.

This book did pretty well, and it got talked about a lot. It generated a lot of word of mouth. And let's think about why something like this would generate word of mouth. Well, one factor is emotion. It's funny. Things that are emotional often are more likely to spread. The second biggest driver, I would say, is the social currency. If you share something that's entertaining, that is surprising, that's funny. There is a currency that's generated there that makes you look good, it makes you seem more likable and makes you seem funny, you kind of get a little bit of credit for sharing something that's hilarious. And I talked about this when I first heard about this book.

And I know it made me look cool because I was showing how an entrepreneur can be successful writing a book that contains nothing in it. So these are some of the factors to consider. You may apply these to your industry for not working in the book industry. But the other thing that you can do with a lot of different markets is you can actually write books to help promote your business, whatever business you're in, and whether that software or manufacturing or any group of people that you want to have influence over a book can can help give you credibility and a book can help go viral. 57. Beard Bib Example - Virality Startups can't pour thousands of dollars into TV ads to build brand awareness the way large B2C companies can.

They can, however, make humorous YouTube chapters and build awareness by appearing on popular TV shows such as Shark Tank. Beard King did exactly this to promote their Beard Bib. One of the biggest challenges with startup marketing—particularly with B2C—is that your CAC ("customer acquisition cost") is quite high. You haven't yet established the economies of scale to do efficient advertising. So startups are tapping into the viral qualities of humorous chapters to acquire customers cheaply through the leverage of word-of-mouth marketing. It may just sound like a fun hobby to create silly chapters, but these are actually smart investments.

Small companies can also piggyback off of the credibility of larger brands such as news outlets and the show Shark Tank. Beard King is a realistic example of how a small company can build initial sales through focusing on chapter. A more stellar example would be Dollar Shave Club which has come to compete with the marketing goliath Procter & Gamble.

The 3 Principles of Growth Hacking

These are the three big principles of growth hacking, you can use these principles to evaluate whether your growth hacking ideas have the potential to produce an exponential return on investment. The first principle is supply and demand. The second is economies of scale or leverage, and the third is marketing psychology. Now, you may be asking yourself. I thought growth hacking was all about rapid testing. I thought it was all about being agile. I thought it was all about getting data and feedback from the market and making quick changes. That's true, and that type of execution can actually be applied to each of these three principles. For example, with supply and demand, let's say you're trying some different low supply channels, one of those might be Tick-Tock, where perhaps there aren't a lot of competitors yet.

You can try it out and if it doesn't work, you can change and try a different channel. And if that next low supply channel works out, you double down on it. And let's look at economies of scale or leverage, what you can do is you can try different key influencers to disseminate your message in whichever one acquires users for you at the lower cost. That's the one you double down on and form an exclusive relationship with the last principle, marketing psychology. You can try different tactical elements, for example, a timer to create time scarcity, see if that outperforms or underperforms another form of scarcity, such as showing inventory shortages.

The other key thing to keep in mind is that these principles in general exist on a time scale. So, for example, marketing psychology techniques tend to give you a short term advantage. Psychology techniques are easy to mimic in the market so competitors can start using it. And then when the market is oversaturated with those psychological techniques, they tend to become less effective. In the midterm, advantages often come from being in markets that are undersupplied or where demand is growing so quickly that effectively you are under supply.

And typically, these types of advantages give you some mid-term benefits, but it's not sustainable because eventually competitors are going to realize that there is a shortage of demand and they'll start filling it one way or another. Often this is particularly beneficial when your competition is larger companies. And if you're a small, agile startup, you have an advantage over large companies that cannot move quickly. They can't move quickly because in order to make changes, they have to go through a lot of political bureaucracy and they also have to be very conservative and be concerned with such things as is this the legally correct approach to take and is it going to work in all international markets in which they are participating.

Now, the last is the long term, and this is where economies of scale or leverage give you a sustainable advantage over your competitors. And the reason for this is because some markets are only large enough to support a few or in some cases one supplier at scale. Now, at the strategic level, that's a fundamental sustainable advantage, being the only supplier in a market or in a duopoly, something like that. But it also applies when we're talking about marketing tactics. For example, in some markets, some niche markets, there's only enough room really to have one major key influencer who dominates the share of voice.

So if you're able to get in early and secure an exclusive partnership with that influencer at the marketing communications level, then you have a sustained share of voice in the market. That's going to be very difficult for competitors to replicate and is going to make for a very successful growth in the long term.

Example of the 3 Growth Hacking Principles

I'm going to show you a quick little example of a growth hacking tactic. This isn't something huge. You don't need a ton of venture capital to do this sort of thing. Anybody that's even just selling their own book or a tiny product can do it. But so could a company with a lot of funding. And what it does is it demonstrates the three principles that we've been talking about. And I've also uploaded it to the Book chapter as a downloadable resource. So we have this person who's making a social post saying my ninety six year old grandpa has just had his own book published with all his poems from his life. It's available on Amazon. If anyone is interested, Smiley faces a review and makes him so happy. So one of the big challenges with selling stuff on Amazon is getting reviews. And Amazon has really cracked down on disingenuous reviews.

And you can pretty much only review a product if you've spent at least 50 dollars. And I imagine Amazon's going to get even more sophisticated with their restrictions. So the fuel that makes this a growth hack is really centered around marketing psychology. It's all about generating social proof. So the more reviews you have, the more likely it is that somebody else will write a review and the more likely it is that somebody will actually buy your product. So what? This person is being very smart. I don't know how strategic she is about this, if it's how intentional it is. But regardless, it's effective and it's something that you can be strategic about. So she's trying to generate social proof reviews, it also has social currency.

So one of the principles we're going to learn later about morality from Jonah Berger is that people tend to share things if it makes them look smart, interesting. Helpful. So this is a heartwarming story and it's a surprising story, it's a newsworthy story. So by sharing it, by reviewing it, you're making yourself look better. You look more interesting by sharing. And I'm not saying that in a distasteful way. It's a genuine desire to want to make others feel good and to to make yourself look like somebody that wants to make others feel good. And the other thing that we have here is emotions. So there's uplifting emotions, inspiring emotions tend to generate vitality and storytelling. It's easy to share stories.

And when stories are embedded in your marketing, there's a high potential there for growth hacking with your tactics. The other key principle is economies of scale. So this isn't about running Amazon ads. It's not about Google ads. It's not about going into some channel and just trying to optimize and tweak your scalability in terms of customer acquisition that we know it's about. Let's do one post that has a lot of emotional appeal. To generate word of mouth and put zero dollars in advertising behind it and then what it does is it becomes self-sustaining because of the word of mouth, because of the sharing, because of the Veraldi nature of it.

You don't need to keep feeding the marketing communications with more funding. OK, and the other thing is supply and demand. So when is the last time you heard about somebody in their nineties or eighties even writing a book? And when and if they did, did you see a photo of it? And even if that happened, was there a young, attractive girl posting the photo? There's a lot that went into this to make it very genuine. You'll notice that there's no capital letters even here. It's just a lowercase I lowercase m. It seems very personal. It seems like this isn't. Trying to manipulate people in any way, it's just a genuine call to action from Jess. So this is not something you usually see.

So it's unusual. It gets noticed because it's undersupplied and unusual stories. If we look at what really gets highlighted in the news, it's not it's not the things you should be worried about most of the time. It's the things that are weird and that stand out because it has shock value. It has an interest. That's the kind of thing that generates publicity. And that's the kind of thing that's generating publicity and growth hacking here. And we can see we got one hundred eighty thousand likes. So, I mean, that's a lot, especially if you're just one guy publishing a book. But, you know, you don't need to generate millions and millions of likes to consider something that is a growth hack.

Obviously, if you're a 20 million dollar company, then that's probably what you need to have any impact. And if your customer lifetime value is very low, you're going to need that. But when you're in startup mode to experiment with viral tactics, one hundred thousand likes is a tremendous achievement. So this is the kind of little thing you can do that applies these three principles.

Supply & Demand Growth Hacking

Supply and demand. Often with supply and demand, what you're really doing is being creative and using contrarian thinking. So this is why a lot of successful growth hackers are nonconformists. These are people who are seeking out opportunities to do things largely because nobody else is doing it and you're going to be able to stand out and get momentum. So some examples of this is to pay people to talk to your sales team. A lot of people are going out there doing marketing, trying to get people to schedule a demo to schedule free consultation. But there are actually very few people out there that are gutsy enough to just say here is one hundred dollars or three hundred, all the electronics items. Please talk to our salespeople, sit through our demo.

Another example is people that are using direct mail, direct mail is not in fashion right now. Generally speaking, what most people like to do is they'd like to use email. They like to do messaging through social media. But if you try something like direct mail, especially if it's very personalized and handwritten, you're going to stand out because these are low supply channels. Another thing that you can do is supply and demand and look for mismatches between supply and demand. So, for example, right now there is an undersupply of audio books. So audible is a marketplace that is undersupplied right now. There's not enough content in contrast to other markets like the Kindle store, which is perhaps a little more mature and saturated.

Other cases are just audio content in general, we're seeing this surge in demand for it with products such as clubhouse, with podcasts. So if you're able to get into that market earlier and ride that wave, you're going to be able to grow your product. Another example is just to follow gen's trends in general and see surges in demand, and there are certain tools like Google Trends that can allow you to do that. And we'll go into more specific examples later in the Book. And another example of exploiting supply and demand is to look where there is cheap labor. So, for example, what you could do is you could hire armies of people in the Philippines that speak English to see the user base for your platform or your product.

Example - Low Supply Growth Hacking

Here's an excellent case study from SACE and to demonstrate the principle of supply and demand and growth hacking. This is a B2B example and there are few things to think about here. So the first is we're looking at a channel that is under saturated right now in business to business, and that is a direct mail gift box. You can see on the left here that there is a very three dimensional mail that goes to the prospective customers. It's not a little letter. It's not a postcard. It's not a flier that you get for a grocery store. It's something big that feels like a gift that you might receive when you're a kid getting a toy or something. So in one respect, the item itself is a form of supply and demand because you're doing something that's surprising and unusual by sending this out.

The second factor that is undersupplied is that there is an incentive for actually doing the demo, doing the conversation with the sales team, and that is this twenty five dollars Amazon gift card. So for those of you that work in business to business marketing, how many times have you ever been actually offered money to talk to a salesperson? It doesn't happen enough, in fact. But that's a great opportunity for you, because if you go out soliciting people saying, hey, I'm going to actually pay you for your time just to talk to my sales team or to talk to me or to do a demo of the product, people are going to respond. They're going to take notice of it. Even if they don't act on it. At least you'll be noticed.

Remembered. I don't know how many junk emails I get on LinkedIn that are just, hey, do you have time for a 15 minute chat? Like nobody, nobody wants to take you up on that offer unless they're highly, highly interested. But people are really going to be receptive to something where you're delivering in an unsaturated way in a way that is more noticeable and more valuable. Now, there's a second way in which this is an undersupplied market, and it's just the fact that it's in Canada. So Canibus, I imagine, is a high growth, high demand, undersupplied market that will probably become saturated over time. It will become more competitive over time.

But in the short term, being in this industry is probably a temporary competitive advantage just by being an early mover. So if we look at the results here, the investment in the mailboxes, the gift boxes themselves was five thousand dollars. Now there are going to be other costs on top of that. So I'm guessing that the labor and the consulting was probably double the cost, probably at least ten thousand dollars plus time, you might say. Let's say let's say the total cost of doing this campaign was fifteen thousand dollars. Well, they generate three hundred thousand dollars in pipeline, which is awesome. Now, the close rate on that might be pretty low.

It might be say twenty five percent. But still you're doing quite well for yourself from a return on investment perspective. And we can see here that the average selling price is twelve thousand dollars per year. And during the same period, three of the sales qualified opportunities already convert it into signed deals. So this is a perfect example of where when you're doing growth hacking, you need to think creative. You need to think about doing things that other people aren't doing. If other people are just blasting the market with cold emails and cold LinkedIn messages, you need to be on the forefront.

You need to think about, OK, this is already saturated. What isn't saturated yet? What are marketers not using? What they're not using a lot of the time is gearboxes, but they're not giving you gift cards to actually talk to the sales team. And then at some point that's probably going to be saturated. So you need to start thinking about the frontier. What are those underutilized channels? What is undersupplied so that I can have a temporary advantage by working with those under supply channels and tactics?

Economies of Scale or Leverage

Economies of scale or leverage. One way I like to think about this is by looking at the finance industry. Specifically looking at people who get rich from investing and one of the key concepts that they use is other people's money. So they get rich largely because they're not limited by the money they have themselves, but they scale by using other people's money. Now, if we look at Warren Buffett, one of the richest people of all time, a lot of people think he got rich by buying undervalued assets. So companies that were very valuable, but the market wasn't recognizing that value. Now, to some extent that's true, but I think the missing ingredient here is the fact that he's using other people's money. What Warren Buffett does is he takes the insurance flow so the premiums that people pay up front for insurance and then he invests those in companies.

So as much as he's good at selecting good investment opportunities, what he's really doing is achieving leverage without needing to borrow money. He's not borrowing money to accelerate his returns. He's using other people's money. Through the insurance flow. A second case where he's using other people's money is when he first started his investment fund. He pulled together money from other people and then invested it on their behalf. So let's go through a few examples of growth hack's. That applies the principle of economies of scale or leverage. The first is word of mouth, so when you launch word of mouth campaigns, there's an initial investment of time and money there, but then there's a cascade effect that sustains the message and spreads the message without you constantly needing to feed the market with content.

Another example is to leverage people who already have massive followings. So there are influencers out there. There are magazines out there, there are YouTube channels out there that have built massive followings over five, 10 years, that will be impossible for you to build organically, very quickly. So what you can do is you can piggyback off of those audiences and growth, hack your product by building relationships and partnerships with those influencers and journalists. Similarly, you can partner with large companies, large companies have spent years, decades even building massive user bases, building trust. Building credibility.

And if you can piggyback off of that, you're going to save yourself a lot of time and effort so that you do not have to start from scratch. Another example of economies of scale or leverage is automation. So, for example, one thing that I do to compile lists, cold lists, is going on to Lincoln and grabbing the emails that are available there. But why do that manually or why pay somebody to manually do it when I can set it on automation using a tool such as scrap that I. Oh, that simply scrapes email page by page. So that I don't have to. Lastly, There's using other people's time in one way to grow. Your product is to focus on user generated content.

Growth Hacking Tactic for Economies of Scale

One of the biggest things to consider when you're trying to grow a product is how do I generate economies of scale or leverage out of this? And I think this is one of the reasons why startups so often fail when they go into products. It's very easy to run a service business, to be a freelancer, to have an agency, to have a consultancy, something like an accounting firm or a marketing advertising agency. It's pretty easy, I would say, because. You're selling high priced products and you're selling your time, there's very little capital investment that's required in that, and you don't need huge economies of scale to reach a satisfying point. The problem is it becomes less scalable over time. You're limited by how much time you can invest.

Now, when it comes to products you're selling typically something that is low priced to a large amount of people instead of something high priced to a small amount of people. And large companies tend to be very good at this because large companies are focused on economies of scale. So they do an upfront capital investment in something such as a product. And what they're able to do is distribute it to a large number of people at a low price. So where it becomes really challenging is when your product is actually free, you have a freemium product, as we see with companies that are doing product-led growth there or free to play games.

There are lots of users using your product that aren't paying anything. So what you need to think about is if you have a bunch of people that are either on your product for free or they're paying a very low price, you need to figure out how to get more value out of each user. And value doesn't need to be financial. It doesn't mean that you need everybody to pay or you need everybody to upgrade to your premium plan. What it means is that you leverage those people to generate more economies of scale, to be able to get more people in your ecosystem, a fraction of which are going to become those premium customers that are going to upgrade.

They're going to buy more products. They're going to buy more small transaction add ons, that sort of thing. And that's what we're seeing with this company chapter. So chapter Champ is a company I recently signed up for just to do some quick, easy chapter editing. I had a chapter that had some poor lighting and I needed something to improve it. And here's this little cute little growth hacking tactic they're using to generate economies of scale. Every time that I save a chapter by default, it says Made with chapter champ, it gets tagged onto the end of every single file name by default. That's something that any startup could implement, especially in the software industry. So what they're doing here is they're saying, hey, maybe maybe you're just on our lower, lower priced plan.

Maybe you're just on like a free trial or freemium. But we're going to use you to generate word of mouth, whether you like it or not, because every time you send a file to somebody, it's going to be tagged with chapter champ. And people are going to think of that name. It's going to build brand awareness so they're getting more value out of users, even though they're at a low price point. Very clever and a great demonstration of how to generate economies of scale or leverage without a lot of investment.

Marketing Psychology Growth Hacking

Marketing, psychology. I'm going to provide a few examples of growth hacks for marketing psychology, and we'll get into more detail later in the Book. One example is to give people options. Now, a lot of marketers and growth hackers out there, they just try to push one call to action. But if you give multiple options, what it does is it makes people take ownership of the decision that they've made, so they're actually more likely to make a decision that's consistent with what you want. So the key here is to present multiple options, all of which are ones that you want people to choose anyways. Another example is setting social proof. So, for example, what you may have is some sort of trigger in your product or on your website that prompts people to write reviews, but only when you've already discovered that they actually love your product.

So, for example, you could have a quick survey or a pop up that just says, do you love our product? Yes or no. And if they say yes, then you funnel them to read a review. If they say no, then you get them to contact your customer support team or something like that. Another thing is to focus on product features that are visible and talked about, even if they don't necessarily provide as much value. So, for example, microphones, USB microphones that are particularly large.

Are often more talked about and are certainly more visible, especially when you see other YouTube channels using it. So you might want to consider emphasizing product features like that and exaggerating them so that you can generate a growth hack. Lastly, there are all different marketing tactics that you can use to create a sense of urgency. And one of those is a timer that you put on your landing page to tell people when the specific offer. Is going to expire.

Example - Marketing Psychology Growth Hacking

When I was growing up, I was indoctrinated with the idea that conformity is bad, you should be an individual who makes your own moral choices. You don't just copy what other people are doing, because if one person walks off a cliff, you shouldn't follow them over the cliff. But one of the most important concepts in marketing psychology is social proof. And it's this fundamental idea that humans are essentially like sheep. We tend to do what other people do, and that's the reality. And nowhere is it more true than when you're certain and you're going to be trying something new. And that's often what you're doing with startup hacking is you are trying to get a bunch of people to use your product for the first time.

And one good demonstration of marketing psychology is linked in Sales Navigator. So I was going to the LinkedIn Sales Navigator page to promote it because I was interested in using it for account based marketing. And they list the benefits, the features. They have some imagery and whatnot. But one of the most interesting things was in the bottom right. They had a customized personalized demonstration of who else I'm connected to. That is using Sales Navigator. I see their names, I see their faces. And I'm like, oh, OK. He uses it. He's successful. All right. Maybe I should, too. So what LinkedIn is doing is they're trying to reduce the risk. So any time somebody wants to buy a product, there is always going to be some sort of objection. It's too risky.

It's too much commitment. What if it breaks? What if it doesn't work? You know, I don't want to be a guinea pig for a new product. So what they probably did in their research is they realized, OK, one of the reasons that people are not buying it is they just don't know if anybody else uses it. Are they getting value out of it? Is it even worth staying subscribed to? But. What this does is it alleviates that perception of risk at the transaction stage on that checkout experience. OK. They use it. All right, I'm going to two so linked in. Great example of applying the principle of marketing psychology for growth hacking.

Growth Hacking Mistakes

I'm going to reveal some big and common growth hacking mistakes. The big one is defining your target market. As the target customer. Your target market is not just the target customer. The target market consists of five different components: customers, collaborators, context, competitors and company. These are strategic decisions, these are not just tactical ones. The two that are the biggest opportunities from a growth hacking perspective are the collaborators in context. So if you're defining your target market as just the customers, you're missing out on the biggest growth hacking opportunities.

So collaborators, these are the big partners, the big companies, the big retailers, the big influencers, the big sources of leverage that are going to empower you to grow extremely quickly without having been around for a long time and having a giant user base. So that is arguably the single most important source of growth. The other is context. So these are things like environmental changes that are happening in the market that provide huge opportunities for you. So if something is trending, if there's going to be an abrupt change, you're in a favored position, especially if you're a smaller company, because you're able to satisfy whatever that changing need is based on those environmental conditions, faster than incumbents are going to be able to because large incumbents tend to move very slowly.

The next is building scalable systems before first getting market feedback. So, for example, you make it all excited about a partner program. Now, I'm huge on partnerships. I think it's one of the most undervalued sources of growth. However, if you haven't. Being able to develop some sort of pilot program with those partners that you're thinking about partnering with, you're not going to have enough information to invest in a partner program and the partner program itself may fail. The other thing that you may find is that you don't actually need one hundred partners. So why invest in this giant affiliate system if it just means you're going to need to manage relationships with all these tiny partners that are not going to bring in a lot of customers, are not going to bring in a lot of leads.

So instead of investing in something like a giant partner program, just build something that's not scalable at first, do it manually, do it one to one, do it through manual outreach, through email, through LinkedIn, et cetera, get a pilot program going, get some feedback. And then later on, if you see that as successful, see it's getting traction, then you can worry about it becoming scalable. Now, relate it to this topic of scalability when companies invest in large capital sunk costs too early. Now, this might be a bit contradictory because earlier I was talking about how economies of scale are one of the big sources of growth.

Hacking and investing in large capital costs is one of the ways that you achieve economies of scale. But when you're too young, when you're not big enough, instead, what you should be doing is borrowing leverage by working with companies that already have the scale, by working with the influencers that already have the clout, by working with PR agents who have connections to people that have a lot of visibility in your target market. So one example of this I find is there's this inherent idea, particularly with micro startups. There's a lot of content in this Book that's going to be relevant to medium and large companies as well.

But if we're talking about really tiny companies, one of the first things they think is I need to spend thousands of dollars on a website, let's say five, ten thousand, twenty thousand dollars on a website. You don't need a website to acquire customers, for example, and business to business. You could just launch an ad campaign on LinkedIn, a lead generation campaign where you don't send people to a website. All you do is capture their information through a lead form. On LinkedIn itself, you could send a cold email campaign just to start conversations. So it's exciting to obsess over these ideas of having a fancy website, this thing that is a bit of an ego boost. But you need to focus on the core of where the growth is coming from.

Growth is not coming from your website. It's going to come from conversations with the sales team or it's going to come from people hitting that by now button. And sometimes all that means is advertising emails, phone calls, marketing systems that really don't have much to do with the website at all. And even if you do need a website, sometimes all it is is a landing page, a one page promo to sell your product or to generate leads. OK, another thing, and I think this is particularly true with growth hackers who are already experimenting in the market, they self identify as growth hackers. They obsess over attribution and analytics. This is a huge sin that a lot of marketers are falling under.

And one of the main reasons for it is that it gives marketers credibility, especially when they're working with CFOs and CEOs who want to see that there's a clear ROIC. There's a clear financial impact here. But the problem is that a lot of the growth hacking methods that produce the biggest impact are not going to be ones that are easy to measure and be able to attribute things like lead generation to. So often what people end up doing is they end up focusing on all these tactics that are easy to attribute and easy to measure, but really don't produce much impact. The impact is linear rather than exponential. Now, there's a whole series of reasons for this. One is that attribution tools out there are only able to measure things that are digital, that are online.

And as we know, and as I'll talk about later on, word of mouth is mostly offline and offline is inherently more difficult to measure now that there are certain tricks that you can use to measure them. But measurements are not really. The focus of measurement is something you do after there are effects. But the focus initially is the causes. What is causing people to change their mind? What is getting them excited to use your product? Who is the person that's endorsing your product? So examples of this are podcasts. Sport podcasts are a great way to build excitement awareness for your product, but they're also very difficult to measure. So often what we see is that in tactics where there is oversaturation, where there are too many companies using them.

Those are the very ones that are easiest to integrate with distribution tools. And those are the exact ones that you don't want to be using when you're a growth hacker. You want to be using the ones that other people are not using. And often those are going to be ones that are more difficult to measure. OK, lastly, this is one of the big mistakes obsessing over vanity metrics, and I'm going to focus here on business to business. We have here a typical marketing and sales funnel that business-to-business companies use. This from Forrester Research. And often what marketers do is they become very obsessed over NKL, some marketing qualified leads.

I define these as people requesting demos or requesting sales conversations, perhaps people that are signing up for free trial. Often marketers will focus even earlier in the funnel on murky marketing, captured leads or marketing engage leads. So these are things like people who provide you their email address to download a white paper order to register for a webinar. If you obsess too much over these, what you're going to end up doing is what most business to business marketers do, which produces tons of leads that never convert to customers. If only one percent of your so-called leads are converting to customers, you've got to ask the question, was that even worth it? So instead, what you should be emphasizing is deeper into the funnel.

So things like sales, qualified leads, things like pipeline revenue or sales, qualified opportunities and things like acquiring customers. Now, don't get me wrong, I think you do need to focus on these top funnel metrics, particularly with product led growth, where you're trying to get the user base as large as possible. But just be cautious and don't delude yourself into thinking that because you paid twenty dollars for an individual or missile or whatever, that that's a predictor of a paying customer. OK, don't get too excited about vanity metrics. Make sure you're holding yourself accountable to the real metrics that matter.

Look for Big Opportunities, Not just Problems

A lot of people, when they are trying to come up with business ideas or they're trying to come up with marketing campaign ideas. The crux is the problem, they start with a problem that they have or that somebody else has, and then the supply side is solving that problem. This approach is great. It solidifies your chances of success because you know that there is a real value proposition there. So it's better than starting with a product concept. OK, let's just come up with an invention or something and then retroactively try to figure out what problem to solve with that. So in general, problem focused thinking is effective. With growth hacking, however, you may want to consider a different approach, because with growth hacking, what we're trying to do is get growth really quickly by taking the problem.

First approach, you will have a viable business, you'll have a viable product, but there's no guarantee that it'll ever become something that explodes. So what we're looking for is explosive opportunities, things that are rapidly changing and then riding that wave as a growth hacker. The best example of this is Amazon. So Amazon didn't start with the idea that, hey, I can't buy the book that I want, I can't find it. No, Amazon started with Jeff Bezos looking at this huge boom that's happening, this Internet thing, and then thinking, OK, how do I exploit this big opportunity, this big trend? So then he starts looking at various industries and figures out, OK, what I'm going to do is I'm going to sell books.

So the beginning of his rationale is where is the big opportunity? And then figure out the details of what problem I'm going to solve or what I'm going to supply the market with. So some big opportunities that are happening right now are tick tock, tick tock suddenly becomes this huge thing. So as a marketer or a business person, you might start thinking, OK, how do I latch on to this trend? And it might mean selling books on tick talk marketing. Or it may mean just doing marketing through tick tock as a channel. There are lots of ways that you can exploit opportunities like that.

Now, clubhouse is another example, so we're seeing that there are these big opportunities that are sprouting up in audio in general, we're thinking about devices that Amazon's putting out, we're thinking of podcasts. But then suddenly this clubhouse thing comes up. Is this kind of revolutionary concept in social media? So you can start thinking about maybe I could dominate that market. I could be the number one. Marketing clubhouse, or I could use clubhouse as a way to suddenly spur my content marketing or I could build an integration with clubhouse.

So there are different aspects to this on the product side, on the marketing side, where you're able to exploit a trend. I was talking to a colleague of mine who built a multi-million dollar software business and one of the key chapters that he learned from failing was certain products that he built failing with certain marketplaces and succeeding with others. Is this quotation you want to integrate with a market that is growing? So if you're early and enter into an app store or into a marketplace, you've established yourself and that's a growing market, you're going to have a bit of at least a temporary competitive advantage as that system grows, as the user base grows.

So the question is, how do you find these trends? Well, you can go to websites like Tread Hunter, you could go to Kaura, start asking questions, you can go to Facebook groups, et cetera. But what we're doing is we're trying to think more macro in terms of trends and less micro in terms of specific problems. And Of course, you can use Google Trends to figure out and dive more deeply into specific categories that you're interested in exploiting. So, for example, here we see the word inclusive has had rapid growth in the last 12 months in terms of search volume. So maybe there's an opportunity to sell clothing that's more inclusive, to do things that are more inclusive, to build campaigns around exclusivity or any keyword that you find that's trending.

Growth Hacker Marketing

One of the single easiest and simplest marketing hacks to implement. Is to simply pay people. To talk to your sales team. And by paying them, I mean cash or a gift card or some sort of product that that individual would value, not talking about the organization, not some sort of special incentive that the company would appreciate, but something that the individual that you want to talk to the salesperson. Would value. This is most applicable when you're marketing a large business to business products or services. Because the transaction size is so large that it makes sense to pay a large amount of money to get somebody to talk to the salesperson. It also makes sense because often high level manager CEOs, et cetera, are very busy people. Their time is valuable. So it makes sense to pay those people for their time.

However, I believe that these techniques are also effective when you're dealing with small businesses and there are ways to adjust it so that it's suitable for consumers, for example. You might just go with a smaller incentive for consumers, just pay them, say, five dollars or something like that. The other thing that you can do is you can have a sweepstakes. So while you're not paying individual consumers to talk to your sales team, what you are doing is paying one out of every, let's say, 10 in the lottery system so that one person gets some sort of big payoff and the others get a chance for a big payoff. It's surprising how few marketers take this. Paying people to talk to the sales team. It's similar to what I see with list building or lead generation in general.

What people do is they have a preference for indirect ways of solving problems. Which is really an anomaly to me, if you want an end result, why don't you take the shortest possible path to get it? So with leads, people that come up with lead bait lead magnets to try to entice people to give you their email address. They do search engine optimization. They do Google as they do all sorts of these little tactics and tricks to capture people's email addresses. But the fastest route to get somebody's email address or contact information is just to buy a list. You can just go to a list broker, you can go to Info USA, go wherever and get the list. Then you don't need to spend 12 months compiling a list of people and running ads to lead magnets when you could just directly pay for the contact information yourself.

Marketers have a bias towards indirect routes to things, and often it's a form of procrastination. So if I'm busy capturing leads, capturing contact information, I don't have to do the actual hard part of marketing, which is convincing somebody to buy. It's easy to convince somebody to give you their contact information. You just give them some sort of reward incentive, something that would be highly valued. The hard part is the nurturing and the persuasion of getting somebody to buy. Now, similarly here with getting somebody to talk to the sales team, you can do all sorts of convoluted things to trick people into requesting a free trial or registering for a webinar. And then suddenly they're in a conversation with the sales team that they never ask for. OK, that's it.

In an indirect way of trying to get a conversation with the salesperson, the most direct way to approach the target customers, the target personas and just say here, here's some money, listen to our sales pitch. And if it's valuable, they'll buy from you. Once you get in front of them and you have something valuable and you're able to convince them they'll buy. But if you don't, it's just not going to work. So consider this direct route, consider this as a general rule of thumb with growth hacking is to look for opportunities to go directly for what you want instead of these indirect, convoluted routes that most people take. One of the main things to consider here is that people's time has value.

Especially when you're marketing to say doctors, high level executives, fortune, five hundred directors, these people are paid very highly on an hourly rate. So you. Should compensate them for that time. And I see this all the time with marketers. In fact, one of the most common questions I get or that I see in the marketing communities that I belong to is nobody responding to my survey research. Nobody wants to volunteer to do interviews with me. And it's that their time is valuable. You're asking somebody to give you something for free. Yeah, OK. They're not giving you their time for free. They're not giving you an excuse. They're not giving you money for free or the product for free. But you're asking them to give up 30 minutes.

Forty five minutes, whatever of their time. Absolutely free. Which is a bit of an absurd concept in business when people sell their time for one hundred two hundred dollars an hour, why should they just volunteer that for you? So if you want people to talk to your sales team, you want them to sit down and hear your sales pitch. And you want them to overcome the switching costs of switching to your product, then just pay them to be able to deliver your presentation. Simple, simple concept. The other thing to consider is that one way or another, you're paying to acquire customers. Most obvious example is you're running Google ads, you're sending people to a landing page.

A certain fraction of people are going to actually convert after they click your ad, so you're paying for every click and then only a fraction of those people are actually going to sign up for whatever your offer is. A fraction of those people are actually going to sign up to talk to the salespeople. And then an even further fraction of those are actually going to show up to the sales conversation. The people that do show up to the sales conversation may not be qualified, so they're not going to become opportunities. And then of those that become opportunities, only a fraction of those are going to become paying customers.

And then a fraction of those aren't even going to be profitable customers, so the more you go down the funnel, the more you realize that that top of the funnel is. Incredibly inefficient in general across marketing communications that are running across multiple companies, only a tiny fraction of leads actually end up converting into paying customers. So one of the easiest ways around that is to just pay directly for that demo, that free consultation, that conversation with the sales team. And then you're able to bypass all the wasted nonsense at the top of the funnel. You're able to pinpoint the exact type of customer that you want. You want fortune. Five hundred tech.

Chief technology officers, senior directors, whatever, go after them, pay them to sit in here, your sales pitch. One of the reasons that marketers run into this problem is that they're optimizing for leads. They're optimizing their budget for how many people register for a webinar, how many people download a white paper, how many people sign up for a free trial? But what they're not necessarily doing is optimizing for customer acquisition cost and for lifetime value, which are basically the furthest thing you can get away from vanity metrics. These two variables right here. So as you start to think about customer acquisition, cost is the true measure of performance, then it starts to make sense to pay people to sit through your demo.

So let's say that the incentive is a fifty dollar Amazon gift card. Well, you might be like, wow, I can run some Facebook ads and generate leads for 50 dollars. Why would I pay for direct mail? And on top of that, a 50 dollar Amazon gift card to capture a lead or get somebody to respond. I can just use Facebook. That's the problem with that line of thinking, is that you're not going deep enough into the funnel. Only a percentage of the people that convert for your Facebook at Google and whatever are actually going to become paying customers. So you may be able to afford three times the amount you're paying for it on Facebook.

With an incentivized offer that you send through perhaps email perhaps, or direct mail to get somebody to actually sit through a demo because you're getting people that are further down in the funnel and there's a high chance that they're going to be more qualified as well, because you're going to be more focused on your ideal customer profile when you're actually paying them to sit through a demo. It's constraining you to focus on people that actually have a high probability of buying from you instead of inflating vanity metrics like top of funnel leads. So I'm going to walk you through a few examples of where this has been effective. Most of these are coming from Sarsae and Cuil websites.

You should check out some great case studies. So what we have here is a direct mail box and the reason that they're sending a box is because it's the least likely. Marketing assets to get thrown out. If I send a postcard, there's a high chance that the receptionist or somebody is going to filter it out, throw it away. If you send a letter and it looks like spam, it's going to get thrown out. Less likely to get thrown out if it's handwritten, but something that's big and bulky like this. Very, very low probability, somebody will just throw that out, so you'll notice that there are a few things here. There's some food, there is a postcard in here. There's information written on the box. Now, the thing that I really want to highlight is that there's this offer of a 50 dollar Amazon gift card.

And then what they're doing is they're pushing people to a landing page. And on the right side of the landing page is the scheduler to get the demo, get the demo booked, and then if the person sits through the demo, they're going to get a fifty dollar Amazon gift card. And sometimes what happens in this case is that they're motivated by the offer or the special incentive, which is the Amazon gift card. The nomenclature gets a little bit confusing because when you use this approach to demand generation, you have the offer, which is the demo or the sales conversation, and then you have a second offer, which is the Amazon gift card.

So what you may want to do is call the second offer an incentive. But this is just a linguistic adjustment that you can make. So this is effective in generating a million dollars in sales pipeline, using direct mail and using these basically paying people to sit through a sales conversation. We'll walk through some other examples and show what this looks like from a return on investment perspective instead of just a revenue perspective. Here is another case where the offer being sent is not a special gift card, what it is, is a bottle of wine and the results here. OK, so they target 250 prospects to target accounts, the campaign cost about nine thousand dollars and the revenue generator, the pipeline revenue generated was about one point five million.

Sending out direct mail with a special incentive as a bottle of wine, now that is incredible. So, Of course, pipeline revenue is actual revenue. So this is the revenue, potential revenue that's associated with sales, and qualified opportunities. Probably about a third of this would become paying customers. So maybe five hundred thousand. But even then, at a campaign cost of nine thousand plus, I'm sure there's a lot of labor time that went into that. So even if we doubled it and said it was, say, twenty thousand dollars total to launch this campaign, five hundred thousand dollars in incremental revenue, this is incredibly profitable. This is direct mail with incentives to get people to actually sit through your sales conversation. Excellent, excellent growth.

Another example, we have a special mail out with an offer of an I read. So if this executive. Sit through a conversation with Proofpoint, they get. This read is for free and sometimes what happens is they are all excited about the special incentive, the read in this case, and then after the end of the demo, if they're actually excited about your product, they may even forget about the incentive that motivates them in the first place. So, you know, I'm not saying you should depend on this, but in a lot of cases, you may not even actually need to deliver the incentive that you use to get them in the door. But, Of course, you fulfill your promises. And I'm not saying deceive or anything, but just keep that in mind.

Now, the last example I'm going to show here is from this company, Open Rice, and what they're doing is AB testing. They're AB testing. By changing the incentives, so the demo, the offer itself, the main offer is the same, it's a demo of Open Eyes and then there's some tax call to action, et cetera. But what they're really testing is, would both speakers outperform Amazon gift cards as an incentive to get somebody for a demo? And that's something you can test. You can say we're going to try some flashy new electronics item versus just cash or we're going to try and offer to donate money to a charity that we know that person likes.

So if you're really doing account based marketing and honing in on the individuals in that buying group and you know them very well, you may know that they sit on the board of a charity or something like that, and you can offer to make donations there. There are different testing that you can do, but if you. Aren't scaling this up yet, and you're just playing around, I was just just starting with something like an Amazon gift card or just the cash itself, like a PayPal payment, something like that.

Pay People to Talk to Sales

Regeneration is actually incredibly easy. The reason that marketers believe regeneration is difficult is because the way they go about it is wrong. They go about regeneration in a very indirect way. So, for example, marketers will spend a lot of time writing thought leadership pieces, writing blog posts, writing long pieces of content that are interesting, that position the company well, but really do not move the needle when it comes to lead generation. And the reason is because those kinds of tactics are not explicitly designed to generate leads. So I'm going to give you an example of why it is incredibly easy to generate leads. The first is that you simply buy the leads, you go and you buy the list, you can get it from a list broker, you can get it from somebody who solicits you via email to purchase a list and you can browse the Internet.

So, for example, here's a company called—with Pipe Candy. I can go and buy a list of nutraceutical companies, a list of Shopify plus stores, a list of direct to consumer brands. These are Reles. These are not necessarily leads that are ready to speak to your sales team, but they are leads that you can add to your database. I'll give you another example. Info USA, one of the most popular places to purchase leads here. I can decide, do I want a list of leads for businesses, a list of leads for consumers? Let's take an example. Going into the business lists, I can see, oh, I want new U.S. businesses.

I want doctors, I want nurses. We can go deeper to see if there's more specific lists, a list of people that have gone bankrupt, a list of Canadian businesses, dentists, maybe you're selling specialized software or specialized products that dentists want. Well, why go generate a list of leads of dentists if you can just go to Info USA and say, here, here's my money, give me the list, and then a couple of days you have the list instead market or spend a lot of time, a lot of energy, a lot of effort into things that produce leads very slowly. I'm going to give you another example. We do not just have to buy lists, we could also go about buying leads through content syndication so I can go to a content syndication company. This is just an example, pure B2B.

And I can say, OK, I'm willing to pay this much per lead to get people to download my white paper about a problem that my target customer saw. So every time pure B2B sends you leads, you pay them for those leads. So in effect, you are paying for leads through content syndication. I'll give you another example of why lead generation is very easy, you simply give away something for free. So maybe you're at a trade show and you decide we're going to give away a hundred dollars Visa gift card if you show up to our booth or we're going to give you a free stay at a hotel or we're going to give you a free vacuum, we're going to give you our product for a year.

These are ways of getting leads, giving away something for free. What most people do is they give away something like an e-book or a white paper in exchange for contact information. They call that elite. The other way to get more leads is to simply relax your definition of what constitutes a leak, so you loosen it and you say anyone for which we have an email address is considered a lead or anyone that volunteers their information is a lead. The more you relax the definition, the more your number of unknown leads increases. Here's the thing, though. Lead generation, easy, fast, cost effective, you can pay tens of cents for lead. Here's the hard part. It's the lead nurturing. This is what's difficult. It's not generating the leads.

It's the persuasion and the sales tactics that convince somebody not just to be a leader, but to talk to your sales team in some cases if you're selling an expensive product or to buy your product. This is particularly true if you're selling a low priced product. So with the lead nurturing, that's very difficult. And that's the part that most marketers miss, and that's the part where most marketers fail.

Lead Generation Is Easy

One simple growth hack is to look for low supply channels. I'm going to give you a few examples of what these are today, they may not be in the future, but they are to some extent now. The first is direct mail. So these are physical postcards, physical boxes, physical letters that are sent to people's physical addresses. And this is. Basically it has been outdated because people are switching to email, to digital ads, etc., but it used to be very popular. Direct mail used to be a huge focus of the 1980s and 90s, and then it fell out of fashion. So what that presents to marketers today for growth hacking is the opportunity to enter a low supply channel.

So when somebody receives direct mail and they're not used to receiving a lot of direct mail, the way perhaps they're used to receiving email spam or LinkedIn spam, they're going to be more likely to pay attention to it. So it's an opportunity to get noticed in ways where your competitors are not going to get noticed or where the status quo provider isn't present. Another example is Twitter ads for Twitter ads are pretty new. They haven't been around as long as Google ads, Facebook ads. So it's a bit of an undersaturated market.

So if you can master Twitter ads, that will present to you an opportunity where your costs are probably going to be a lot lower than more competitive markets, where a lot of people have already congregated on Google ads and Facebook ads. Similarly with LinkedIn and LinkedIn, ads are not fully saturated right now, I don't think people have fully recognized the value of LinkedIn ads and just how much efficiency is achieved through precise targeting. I don't think people realize that message ads on LinkedIn generate 50 percent open rates, which is incredible. And even though email marketing to some extent is free, the amount of time you need to spend to get people just to actually look at your email is tremendous.

And LinkedIn MessageLabs is one opportunity to enter a fairly low supply channel. And in this case, it's actually pretty. It could become very competitive because people are only allowed to receive a certain number of LinkedIn messages per month. So what this means is early adopters have a huge advantage when you enter a low supply channel as an early adopter, you are going to be able to exploit that market and get basically below market rate or below what the market rate should be in the future as more competitors and suppliers enter that channel and drive up the price. Another example would be handwritten letters. So today everybody is used to seeing text, if you actually.

Take your hand, write a letter, or you use a supplier like a letter friend to manually hand write something with pen or pencil or even crayon, something that stands out, people are going to notice because it's a low supply channel and it's not something that can just be cheaply reproduced. And people value things that they know require time, effort, energy, and personalization. So to give you one example, what we're going to look at is an oversaturated market, which is Google ads. Now, I'm not saying Google ads are not profitable, but in a lot of cases that's oversaturated. And one of the reasons is just because Google has been around for a long time and they've been in the advertising game for a long period.

So when you go and start advertising on Google, you are competing with Fortune 500 companies that are hiring global marketing advertising agencies and they have massive economies of scale. So they may actually be losing money on their campaign in the beginning as they're setting everything up, they're testing things at a wide scale, but in the long run, they just operate at greater profitability than most small businesses possibly can. So when they're paying 20 dollars per click to reach executives, how on earth are you expected to compete against that? So I'm not saying this is always true. I do recommend Google ads and the Google ads are great because they're focused on people that are buying content further down in the funnel.

So often it's an excellent place to start. But if that bottom of the funnel area with Google ads is oversaturated, why not consider going with something like Bing? Or why not consider focusing on channels where you're able to reach people further up in the funnel through something like podcast's? Another example that I want to highlight is content marketing or what HubSpot is calling inbound marketing. So inbound marketing is this idea that if you generate lots of content through things like blog posts, you're able to build up a lot of credibility with your target customers by educating them, by providing them all sorts of ebooks, things like that. Usually we're talking about text based content.

We're talking about this kind of inbound content marketing. And one of the biggest benefits here is search engine optimization. You're going to show up at the top of Google Bing search results because you've produced valuable content that people are consuming. The problem is that a lot of people started doing this. A lot of people started generating tons of blog posts, tons of white papers, tons of ebooks, and soon the market became oversupplied with content. So now it's actually very difficult to just focus on the content marketing machine and get success or at least get success quickly. It takes a lot of time to build momentum.

So with growth hacking, you might want to look for markets that are a bit less saturated. Would you want to look for areas where there is low competition now? When I started teaching years ago, it wasn't the same place that it was today. There weren't as many instructors. There was more flexibility. I was able to have more control over pricing and I made money very quickly. So I think my first Book made like fifteen thousand dollars in just a couple of months. I didn't even really know what I was doing back then, but I had a lot of valuable content to put out there that I knew people would consume. And one of the reasons it was successful, however, was not just that my content heard that I thought my content was great, but just that there weren't a lot of other people doing it.

So when you get in on the ground floor of opportunities like these, you can have a temporary competitive advantage as an early mover. It's not sustainable, but it may be enough to get you to a state where you've been growth hacked and then you can start resorting to more traditional marketing tactics. An example of this today is a company called Soumaré, which provides audio content, bite sized audio content. So everything about content today, typically it's text based blog posts, white papers, etc. There's also chapters that you see on YouTube. There are webinars, podcasts which are long form audio content are kind of the frontier for a lot of companies like Shopify. But you don't really hear much about bite sized audio.

And here's the interesting thing. People can talk about five times faster than they can type. So audio content is very efficient. And there's a reason that when people have meetings, they actually. Talk verbally or meet face to face, because it's extremely fast, it's not as efficient to do something like emailing back and forth, and that gets very irritating for people. So audio content has tremendous value and not everybody wants to do a zoom meeting or a Google meet when maybe they haven't showered, they don't look particularly good or they have kids running around in the background, but they're OK with doing audio. So this is a great opportunity to get into content marketing in a space that has very low supply, and that's with these tiny little easily consumable audio bits.

Kindle Direct Publishing. So there are lots of info printers out there and what they would do is they create engines to produce tons and tons of digital books and they made a lot of money doing this. And the quality wasn't that good. Some of these books were just made with ghostwriters overseas and you just became a publishing machine. But what's happened now with successful Kindle publishers is they're much more focused on very high quality books that they write themselves or they generate a lot of the content and then they get a ghostwriter to put it together. But you see, what's happened is that as more and more writers enter the Kindle marketplace, it becomes more and more difficult as it becomes oversupplied, more competitive, you need to produce higher quality products that can become blockbusters. But initially, it was easy.

It's easy to compete in a low supply market. And we see that at the macro level in the economy. In the nineteen fifties, mid 20th century, we were dealing with a market that had low supply. So all the emphasis was on just producing as fast and efficiently as possible. It was all about the supply chain, it was all about producing things as quickly as you could to get it to market to capture profit. That isn't the game anymore. The market has become. Demand-Driven. There's not a shortage of demand, not a shortage of supply. So as long as the market moves power more towards the demand side, towards the consumer side, then suppliers need to focus more on quality.

They need to focus more on creating products that people want instead of just pushing things out to market and hoping that people will buy them. That macro level thinking is where you're going to see opportunities for growth hacking, because all too often people don't contextualize the marketing tactics that they use and they think, oh, this works or that works. Well, no, that works in a low supply market and this works in a low demand market. So what we're seeing now is the frontier of publishing audible audio books. Kindle has already been through that phase, Amazon in their print books has already been through that phase, but now Audible is just entering that phase where people are starting to produce a lot of content, but those early adopters are going to be more profitable temporarily.

Enter Low Supply Channels: Easy Growth Hacking

You need to stop marketing your product and start doing this one thing that could double your conversion rates marketer offer instead of your product. On the right, you can see some examples of offers and how they are different from products, for example, a consultation, an introductory offer of one percent interest for one year, a free demo, a cheat sheet or a webinar. These are specific offers that the customer receives if they respond to your marketing, direct marketers have known for decades that offer centric marketing outperforms product centric marketing.

Yet marketers continue to promote products with low conversion rates. Tests have proven that response rates increased substantially when your messaging centers on your offer rather than your product. So why are offers so much more effective than promoting your product? One, they create a strong sense of urgency, especially if the offer is only available for a short time. Two, they present a concrete reward that is directly tied to the action you want the customers to take. Now, in contrast, the value that somebody receives from using a product often isn't realized until much further in the future. Three low commitment offers are usually free and don't involve a lot of time or investment, it is easier to get someone to agree to something that doesn't require a lot of commitment and then ask for a larger commitment in the future for reciprocity.

When you give something to a customer for free, they often feel obligated to give you something in return, either buying from you or committing to something later, such as a phone call with a sales rep. Product marketing rarely creates the sense of urgency or scarcity, needing it to drive action, so promote the benefits of your offer instead of the benefits of your product and use offer centric imagery such as photos of your consultation experience instead of photos of your product.

The End

Low ticket marketing. Everybody talks about high ticket offers, so all the marketing gurus like Dan Locke are going to say, you have to sell something very expensive, a high ticket offer. And I follow this advice. When I started out in marketing, I was selling contracts for 1000 to $2000. I was able to get ten x that got it up to around $10,000 to $20,000 per contract. And it made sense when I was marketing a professional service. When I'm essentially selling my time, it makes sense. Let's get the highest possible contract out of that time. But today I make most of my money from low ticket sales, so I make a lot of money, I get royalties, I make money from Amazon and Kindle. I sell one off one hour consulting calls.

My brothers also sell low ticket items. So they've been selling chapter games highly successfully for many years, selling through Walmart, through GameStop, through Steam. Nowadays, when I worked in Silicon Valley, I worked with some really highly successful entrepreneurs who were customers of some of the software I was marketing, and they were selling low ticket products through Amazon, through Shopify, selling things like supplies. So why are people always promoting this idea that you need to sell high ticket offers, that that's the only route to success? Because it's definitely not. Well, the first reason, I believe, is because their customer acquisition cost is just too high. The type of marketing they're doing is where you're generating leads for, let's say, $10, $50, $100.

And if your product is only 60 bucks, well, you're already losing money because the second that you do any marketing beyond the leads. So the cost of the email software, for example, to nurture them, you're just losing money along the way. So what a lot of these people have done is they market low ticket items, but the entire idea is that eventually they're going to upsell them on something more expensive down the line. Well, the kind of marketing I do, the kind of marketing my brothers do, the kind of marketing a lot of successful entrepreneurs do doesn't rely on that upselling, that cross-selling, etcetera.

So number two is they only know how to market directly to customers. So DTC, which is this popular buzzword right now, they don't really know how to do business to business, to consumer, which is a different model where you work with retailers and you work with partners who help distribute your products to more people cheaply. So you look at a lot of highly successful products. Initially they did this Under Armour, did this. You look at the GoPro, did this by getting into Best Buy even when they only had ten people. So a lot of successful product people just didn't need to go directly to customers. They went through channels, which is what I'm doing, which is what my brothers are doing.

Uh, number three is they don't really know how to do mass marketing. They've never done mass marketing. 99% of people out there giving marketing advice are really only concerned with direct response marketing, which is not generally that good when you're selling a low ticket item unless the low ticket item is just part of a marketing funnel where eventually you're going to sell them a $2,000 product or something like that. I've done mass marketing. I was a global brand and product marketing manager for Sony PlayStation, so I'm very familiar with how this marketing is done, because when you're selling a product that's very cheap, it's much more cost effective to do mass marketing than direct response marketing. We do direct response.

You're going to lose money. So what you really need to think about when you're selling a low ticket is about building a brand and

Also by Gaurav Sanjiv Kalangan

Learn Options Strategies Options Basics & Greeks For Stock Trading By Technical Analysis
Bitcoin, Altcoins & ICOs Learn the Basics of Digital Coins from Zero
Time Management This Is How I Work 300 Percent Faster
How To Build And Implement A Winning Pricing Strategy
Networking For Introverts: Gracefully Exiting A Conversation
Accounting 101: Learn Cost Accounting From A To Z
Growth Marketing: Strategy & Execution Bootcamp For Startups

Don't miss out!

Visit the website below and you can sign up to receive emails whenever Gaurav Sanjiv Kalangan publishes a new book. There's no charge and no obligation.

https://books2read.com/r/B-A-EPFBB-ZYDYC

BOOKS 2 READ

Connecting independent readers to independent writers.

promoting a brand rather than just promoting individual cheap products. Because the investment that you put into promoting one individual cheap product is not really going to pay off in a linear way. You run a Google ad and you pay $5 per click and your products 495 you've lost money. But if you do mass marketing where you're able to reach people with a say, ten, $20 CPM and you're able to get thousands, millions of people reading your brand chapter, then the economics starts to make more sense. So the kind of marketing you need to think about is things like how do we build a very memorable brand chapter, something that's entertaining, something that catches the attention.

So for example, I did this recently. I hired an excellent actor to make a very bold ad, and the inspiration for this ad was looking at what worked with Old Spice. They had this fantastic ad, very creative, very unlike anything perhaps you were expecting to see from Old Spice or any brand in this category. So that's the kind of creativity that you want. That's the kind of brand marketing that you want when you're trying to promote a low ticket offer.